WHY GOD GAVE ME PAIN

by Shirley and Susan Holdren
with Candace E. Hartzler

A Campion Book

Loyola University Press
Chicago 60657

"When I Must Leave You," from *Loving Promises* by Helen Steiner Rice, used with permission of the publisher, Fleming H. Revell Company.

Library of Congress Cataloging in Publication Data

Holdren, Shirley, 1939-
   "Why God gave me Pain".

    1. Holdren, Susan, 1959-1980.   2. Lymphoblastic leukemia—Patients—United States—Biography.
3. Suffering—Religious aspects—Christianity.
I. Holdren, Susan, 1959-1980.   II. Title.
RC643.H65H65   1984   362.1'9699'419 [B]   84-11245
ISBN 0-8294-0469-4

Book Design by Carol Tornatore

*In memory of Susan
who taught us hope,
faith and courage*

CONTENTS

FOREWORD

I came to know Susan Holdren, the oldest child of John and Shirley Holdren, while I was serving as pastor of Maize Manor United Methodist Church in Columbus, Ohio. For over two years Susan battled acute lymphoblastic leukemia, while her faith and courage were continually tested and stretched. And there were tears. Tears of fear as she battled her disease, and tears of grief at the end of each remission. But always, even at the worst of times during her illness, she expressed confidence in a God who cares.

Susan was a quiet, reflective, and highly imaginative young woman. She was a gifted artist. Susan was a fighter determined to beat the odds. Her fortitude was admired by all who stood with her during her illness.

A special word of praise is due her family. John and Shirley, sister Brenda, and brother Steven. They, too, walked through a vale of deep darkness as they stood by helplessly watching Susan die. In one of her journal entries, Susan referred to leukemia as a "battle" and a "terrifying death shadow that haunts me night and day, a notorious possessor of life that creeps in and painfully takes over by poisoning my veins with his viper fangs."

Susan's battle ended on March 9, 1980 at 11:45 at night. Her family's battle was then just beginning. Their task is to regroup, to regain their family strength little by little, and to fit the pieces of life's puzzle back together without Susan.

Feeling the words of St. Paul in 2 Timothy 4:7 were appropriate for describing Susan's two year war, I read the following verse at her funeral service:

> I have fought the good fight; I have finished the race; I have kept the faith. Henceforth, there is laid up for me the crown of righteousness, which the Lord, the righteous judge, will award me on that day, and not only to me but also to all who love his appearing.

I leave you to the book. Through it you can gather a greater appreciation of how Susan served as an inspiration to fellow patients, her parents, and to all who came in contact with her.

Rev. Gene Wells, Minister

PREFACE

Susan was born in Mary Rutan Hospital in Bellefontaine, Ohio on April 23, 1959. I was admitted to the
hospital at 4 A.M. on April 22 and wasn't wheeled to
the delivery room until 11:30 that evening. Towards
the end of my pregnancy I had joked with my doctor
about the possibility of the baby being born on my
birthday.

"What do you think, can I expect this baby as a
birthday present?" I had asked while lying on the examining table during my weekly visits.

"Not a chance," he said. "This little one will be
a while yet."

So it was humbly that he awakened me on the
delivery table after positioning the mirror above me,
and said, "Come on Shirley, wake up now, you don't
want to miss this. It's a birthday present you won't
soon forget!"

I was exhausted after the long labor but fought

my way out of a medicated daze to watch Susan make her entry into the world. At 12:07 A.M., just seven minutes into my twentieth birthday, my 6½ pound fuzzy-headed daughter was born.

As a young child, drawing was Susan's favorite hobby. The "Draw Me" pictures appearing weekly in our *TV Guide* were a welcome challenge to her.

Susan grew into a quiet and thoughtful young woman who enjoyed playing musical instruments, developing her own photographs, and drawing with her pencil and sketchpad.

In junior high, art classes sparked a keen interest in her, and by the time Susan reached high school we realized her creativity had grown beyond the hobby stage. She loved doing creative work with her hands: needlepoint, sewing, embroidery, designing and hooking rugs. She began to play the accordian in the third grade, and in later years she graduated to the clarinet, piano, and the guitar just before she became ill.

Sports were another favorite of hers, particularly running on the high school track team. The challenge of running a race, feeling her heart pound as it sent warm blood pulsing through every vein, and being physically exhausted after a victory, were all high points in Susan's young life.

In junior high she came to love Woodstock, Snoopy's aggravating friend in Charles Schulz's comic strip, *Peanuts*. She collected anything she could find with Woodstock's picture on it, and she had over 140 replicas of the little bird when she died. One of her favorites was a plastic version, with yellow fluff on its head and sides. This Woodstock she called "Old Faithful," and she took it with her each time she was admitted to the hospital.

Susan was a religious person who was active in church, studied the Bible, and rarely missed reading from her Daily Devotion book. As her illness progressed, she became even more devoted to reading and studying the Word of God. She received much comfort in her last days by listening to family and friends read her favorite verses from the Bible.

Although cancer stalked Susan night and day for more than twenty-four months and reduced her strong healthy body to a mass of weakness and pain, it was not the victor. For it did not touch her soul. Her soul was as bright and pure as the day she was born because she was at peace with God and at peace with herself. In two short years Susan conquered more feelings of hopelessness and despair than most of us meet in a lifetime.

And Susan fought well. She searched courageously inside herself, asking why, and she courageously reached to God, asking why. She found her answers, and found peace.

This book is intended to acquaint you with the validity of an ever-present God, with the spiritual and emotional growth of a dying young woman, and with the joy and sorrow I experienced while I shared my daughter's last two years.

Shirley Holdren

1

HOW IT BEGAN

"This is ridiculous," Susan said many, many times during the spring of 1977. "These aches and pains are ridiculous. Is this what happens when you graduate from high school; you begin falling apart?"

She would laugh then, and the phrase, "This is ridiculous," became a family joke. We tossed it back and forth among us light-heartedly. Looking back now I realize how important those words became, a shield between us and fear. As long as Susan was teasing her sister, Brenda, about leaving clothes strewn around their room, or later when she laughed while looking in the mirror at her shrinking body in clothes that used to fit and say, "This is ridiculous!" dreary thoughts about the possibility of a serious illness were pushed to the back of our minds.

Susan was eighteen years old then and a senior at Brookhaven High School. Since she was running track that spring, we attributed the pain in her joints to physical exertion. "This is ridiculous," Susan would say after a meet, as she rubbed her arms and legs. "I'd better not run so hard next week."

But we couldn't make sense out of the continuing pain. She was athletic. She loved swimming, volleyball, bicycling and softball in warm weather, and hiking and sledding in the winter. She had always enjoyed good health; strenous activities had never bothered her before.

As a young child, Susan had somehow skipped the usual childhood maladies—chickenpox, measles, and so forth—and thus had little experience with being sick. The nagging aches and pains in her joints were nothing but an aggravation at first. But as spring drifted into summer and the pain increased in intensity, when it became painful for her to make any move at all, when even getting out of bed in the morning became a challenge, we convinced her to see a doctor. And then the headaches began. Susan referred to them as "bells clanging continually in my ears."

I made an appointment for her with our family doctor. Aside from her sinuses acting up (the headaches) and perhaps a little arthritis in her shoulder (joint pain) he found nothing to be alarmed about. He referred her to an orthopedic surgeon, who took x-rays of her joints.

We had to wait two weeks for the results of the tests and x-rays. My husband, John, and I had been planning a trip to the West for several years. Realizing how quickly the children were growing up, we had thought the summer before Susan began college would be a good time for an extended family vacation.

And so, because the children were looking forward to the trip, and we had to wait two weeks for the test results anyway, because we believed our family was immune to tragedy, and because Susan insisted she felt up to it, we left home on August 5, 1977 for a hurried two-week tour of Utah, Arizona, Colorado, South Dakota, and Wyoming.

Susan was sick most of the trip. The headaches and joint pain became complicated by nausea, and we often pulled over to the side of the road for her to vomit. Not wanting to miss any of the beautiful scenery, Susan lay in the back of the station wagon with her head propped on pillows watching the passing mountains and blue skies. She wished she were strong enough to capture their beauty in her sketchbook. She did manage to take some photographs, black and white, so she could develop them in John's darkroom.

When we arrived home, Susan went to the orthopedic surgeon; he asked her to have some blood tests done at the lab. It took another two weeks before he told her to go back to her family doctor; the problem was out of his field.

In September Susan started classes at Ohio State University and put off going back to the doctor. Although she continued to lose weight, felt tired all the time, and was still having those banging headaches, she stubbornly persevered, trying to maintain normalcy in her life.

That fall Susan became a Little Sister in Delta Chi Fraternity, worked part-time at Angela's Pizza, kept up with her studies, and dated a boy named Dave. In December she began to have pain in her wisdom teeth. Feeling that perhaps we had now located *the* trouble spot and had found the reason at least for her headaches, we had her wisdom teeth extracted. Our hopes plummeted, though, when after her teeth were removed and her gums were healed, the headaches persisted.

So Susan went back to our family doctor in

January, 1978. He prescribed medication for her sinuses and told her to come back if she didn't feel better soon. During the next few weeks, the lymph nodes in her neck began to swell, so she made another appointment with the doctor. On the day of that appointment the Blizzard of '78 struck Columbus, Ohio, crippling the city and outlying areas with snow, high winds, and freezing temperatures. The doctor's receptionist called Susan the next day to reschedule her visit, but she was unable to work her in for at least another ten days.

Dave, Susan's boyfriend, had suggested that she go to the University Clinic or emergency room after class the following Monday. Susan fully intended to visit the emergency room that day, but she felt so bad after class it was all she could do to get home and collapse in bed. Finally on Tuesday, January 31, after her eleven o'clock class, she walked across campus through the snow and slush to the emergency room at Ohio State University Hospital.

At three o'clock my phone rang. It was Susan.

"Mom, would you please call Angela's and tell them I'll be a little late for work tonight? I'm supposed to be there by five, but it doesn't look like I'll be finished here for awhile; these guys are being pretty thorough."

She sounded a little tired, but there was an upbeat lilt to her voice.

"They'll find it, Mom. With all these tests I know they'll find the cause of all this pain," she continued.

I felt reassured; she was in capable hands and at last we would *know*. At five o'clock Susan called again; this time she handed the telephone to the doctor.

"Mrs. Holdren, we have a few more tests to administer, and we are admitting Susan to the hospital

4

for the night. She'll be in room 1079." His voice was crisp and professional, concerned but not grave. Apprehension clutched at my insides, and I fought to stamp out the premonition of trouble in a remote corner of my brain.

Room 1079. That was the tenth floor. The cancer floor. The floor where John's sister and uncle had fought, and lost, their battles with leukemia. But perhaps there was a mistake. The other floors could be full and there just happened to be an empty bed on the tenth. Of course.

I gathered a few of Susan's things, just enough for an overnight stay. John and I took them to the hospital. She was tired but very serene when we walked into her room. There seemed to be no doubt in her mind that the doctors would locate the trouble, prescribe treatment, and she would be back to feeling like her old self very soon. Her spirits were up and we buried all negative feelings, at least for the night.

We met with Dr. Chris Gordon who unknowingly made my heart soar when she said, "Susan doesn't have enough white cells. Could be a cat or dog allergy; we'll know more tomorrow."

I remembered Ginny, John's sister, having the opposite problem, not enough *red* cells. So it wasn't as bad as we figured. But I didn't know there were different types of leukemia.

Susan was concerned about leaving her car on campus, so John offered to drive it home. "Thanks, Dad, that will save me from getting a ticket. Oh don't forget to take my paints out of the car or they'll freeze!" she said as we walked out into the hall.

5

2
DISCOVERY AT LAST

I was due back at the hospital at one o'clock to learn the test results. My husband, John, was a part-time professional photographer then and had a customer in a hurry for a black and white glossy print; so I was down in the darkroom at ten o'clock in the morning on February 1, when the phone rang.

Not even thinking that the call would be from the hospital, I was provoked at its persistent ringing in the quiet of the room. I quickly grabbed the picture from the developer tray, dropped it in the fixative solution, and groped my way to the phone. A student doctor from admitting was on the other end of the line.

"Mrs. Holdren, we have finished all the tests on Susan," he said. Timing the picture floating around in the fixative bath, I attempted to concentrate on his voice.

"Your daughter has acute lymphoblastic leukemia."

I remember dropping the picture into a rinsing tray with my heart pounding so hard that it hurt. Standing there alone in the dimly lighted room, I tried to comprehend the gravity of what the young man was saying.

"Childhood leukemia . . . , best kind she could have . . . , easiest to treat . . . , ninety percent chance of complete remission."

There must be a mistake, I thought to myself. My mouth felt full of cotton, and I began to tremble from the inside out. "Did you tell her?" I asked.

"Yes, and she took the news really well."

I felt the air rush from my body as if I was a punctured balloon. I sank to the floor, asking the doctor to repeat the name of the leukemia. As I hung up the phone, I leaned over broken against the counter.

"Is this the way they tell people?" I murmured to myself. "Over the telephone?" On television there was always a dramatic scene in the doctor's office . . . I managed to make my way upstairs to the kitchen where I sat dazed, trying to make sense of the news and trying to decide what to do next.

"John. I must phone John." My mind slowly began cranking messages. For a few minutes I had a purpose. I phoned John at work, and he said he would come right home and go to the hospital with me. He works out of town, so I knew it would be at least an hour before he arrived. Feeling the first tremors of panic, I knew I had to talk to someone while I waited, or else I would shatter into a million pieces. I prayed while I dialed Carolyn's number. "Please God, let her be home." She was home. My good friend Carolyn Callaghan became my stabilizer for the next hour, and for the next twenty-four months.

"Do you want me to come over, do you need someone with you?" she asked.

"No. I just need to talk while I wait for John." Never before had I drawn such comfort from a voice on the other end of the line.

"Maybe it's not as bad as it seems, Shirley. Wait until you get to the hospital and talk to Susan and the doctors," she repeated. Allowing those words to soak through my numbed brain, I remained whole until John arrived.

And so the dreadful disease was discovered and the battle was begun. Susan was transferred to the hematology unit that day. Dr. Arthur Sagone was assigned to her case. It was Wednesday, February 1, 1978. When we walked into her room that day, the first thing Susan asked me was, "Mom, how was your visit to the dentist this morning?"

"Susan, how can you think of me with all you're going through?" I said, hoping to break through her brave facade to let her know she didn't have to protect us. It wasn't until the next day, though, that she shed her protective shield and began to cry: "Mom, I can hardly take all this in. Everything is happening so fast, I can't think!"

As I walked down the hall towards Susan's room that morning, a nurse stopped me and asked how I felt about my daughter having leukemia. Offended by her bluntness, I fought my initial impulse to ignore the question. She was invading my mind, my thoughts, my feelings. Private. I wanted her to leave me alone.

"Crying and grieving won't change the diagnosis, so all I can do is try to be supportive of Susan," I said brusquely.

"Mrs. Holdren," she continued while gently touching my arm, "I know how difficult this must be for you, but have you said the word *leukemia* out loud? It may sound odd, but other families have found the more they actually say the word, the easier it becomes to accept."

Her caring advice came back to me as Susan sat crying into the shoulder of my wool jacket. I asked her if she understood the word *leukemia* and if she was willing to fight. "Mom, if you are all behind me, I'll try my best," she answered. Discussing the seriousness of her situation and coming to grips with the diagnosis that very day was, I believe, the beginning of Susan's will to *win*.

She received the first chemotherapy later that same day. Being a novice on the hospital scene, I found myself not even knowing the right questions to ask. A good friend, Joyce Bennett, went to the hospital with me for this first treatment. She is a nurse, and her father had leukemia, so she was familiar with the various anti-cancer agents used in chemotherapy. She was very helpful explaining the procedures, and so forth. The nurse administering the chemo was also very willing to answer any of our questions. She explained each medicine and its side effects. My head spun as I tried to absorb all these new facts.

And I began searching for more information. When I contacted the local Leukemia Society, I found a little booklet that would serve as one of my "textbooks" during Susan's illness. It explained leukemia and chemotherapy in terms that I could understand:

> Leukemia is a disease of the blood-forming organs. In acute leukemia the bone marrow, found in the center of your body's bones, is replaced by abnormal cells so that it cannot produce normally functioning white cells (infection fighters), red blood cells, which prevent anemia, and platelets, which control clotting and prevent hemorrhaging.

10

In chemotherapy treatments, specific types of drugs are administered to destroy or control the growth of cancer cells. The drugs affect the cancer cells by serving as a preventor of division and growing, or by using up the food needed by the cancer.

I was slowly but surely becoming familiar with the disease that would eventually take my daughter's life.

3

THE HELP OF FRIENDS
AND LAUGHTER

Susan's first blood transfusion threw her into more of a panic than her first chemotherapy treatment. It was given to her one night right after visiting hours. She told me the next day that she almost called me to come back, she was so frightened. The prospect of having another person's blood running through her veins, replacing her own, was traumatic. During the transfusion she began to hyperventilate, and the nurse had to give her a calming shot. Blood transfusions continued to be difficult for Susan. Eventually the nurses premedicated her before beginning the procedure.

Susan began to gain a little of her strength back. On her fourth day in the hospital, she asked me to come early to help her bathe; it was hard for her with the IV stuck in her arm. When I arrived on the tenth floor, I found her in the nurse's lounge painting a picture. She was all smiles and looked great. Those good days made our predicament even more difficult to comprehend.

Susan's outward calm and continual concern for others made her many friends in the hospital. Ginny and Liz, nurses aides who were the same age as Susan, began spending their breaks, and any other time they could get free, in her room. They played cards, shared "girl-talk," and walked up and down the hall with her.

Steve Smallsreed, another aide, became a very close friend of Susan's. He was tall and lanky, had coal-black hair and a wit that brightened many dark days for all of us. Being able to joke and laugh with people her own age was a real lift for Susan.

Susan spent her good days in the hospital drawing, painting, and visiting with her new friends. She became acquainted with another cancer patient named Dallas. He was considerably older than she, but they walked up and down the corridor together talking of his grandchildren and her dreams of the future. When she told Dallas of her fear of blood transfusions, he promised, if he was able, to be with her during the next scheduled transfusion. Although he wasn't well enough the next time Susan received blood, he did sit with her during a later transfusion, holding her hand.

Dallas also tried to make light of the possibility of hair loss. "If it does fall out, Honey, it will grow back you know! And besides, things could be worse. What if your ears fell off instead? Now *that* would be something to cry over!" Susan would chuckle then, and kept his words in her memory.

Bonnie Stagakes became a friend of Susan's quite by chance. She was in her early fifties and had suffered a heart attack. When she improved enough to be moved from intensive care, she was moved into Susan's room. Heart patients are normally assigned to another section of the hospital, but those beds were all full.

Bonnie immediately nicknamed Susan "Susie Sunbeam." "She is like a ray of sunshine," she said during one of my visits. "So serene, bright, and full of goodness."

Bonnie was supposed to walk up and down the halls every day to build up her strength. After she was moved to another room, Susan kept track of her and continually encouraged Bonnie to exercise. By setting up a game of rubber horseshoes, Susan helped Bonnie have fun while she got the mild exercise she needed for her recovery.

One day Bonnie came out of her room and found a piece of tape stretched across the floor saying, "Bonnie starts here." Arrows pointed down the hall to another strip of tape which said, "Bonnie turns around." Susan had gotten some tape from the nurses and found a way to make Bonnie smile.

When Bonnie was released from the hospital, she asked Susan for something to remember her by. Susan drew a picture of Woodstock on a paper bath mat and gave it to her.

Susan had been telling her father for weeks that her 1969 Ford Falcon needed a new muffler. We were driving it back and forth to the hospital so it wouldn't sit idle, and she kept reminding him it was about to lose its exhaust system.

"I don't think it's that bad," John would say, a condescending smile inching across his mouth. "Let it fall off first, then I'll put a new one on."

As we were coming home one night from visiting Susan, the muffler fell off with a loud crash right in the middle of West Northbroadway. John got out of the car, threw the muffler in the trunk, and we chuckled as the car roared like a monster all the way home.

The next day, Susan laughed, saying, "I told him so! I'm glad it happened to him and not to me!" That made her day.

Grandma and Grandpa Holdren had sent Susan a fruit basket with a little rubber mouse sitting in the center—they knew she would think up ways to have fun with him. And she did.

One night she stuck the mouse on her water pitcher, then waited patiently for the pharmacy technician to bring her medication. "Keith, would you please pour me a glass of water?" she asked when he strolled into her room. He reached for the pitcher and jumped six inches. Susan laughed. It was so good to hear her laugh and see pink in her cheeks!

"Hey Susan, I thought that was *real*!" he said, as soon as he realized it wasn't.

"That's what you get for always waking me up at night," Susan said. A smile spread across Keith's face, but after that he always remembered to check the pitcher before pouring water.

4

ACCEPTING THE CHANGES

One day Dr. Arthur Sagone came into Susan's room and asked if she was ready to go home. "Oh Dr. Sagone, I'm scared. What if something should go wrong? I feel more comfortable here, at least until my next chemo treatment," Susan answered.

The doctor was a serious man who stood at the foot of her bed with his right hand cupped over his mouth; he was deep in thought. He looked over at me. I shook my head. "OK, Susan," he said, dropping his hand to his side. "We'll give you your next chemo in a few days, then maybe you'll feel more ready."

In between her first and second chemo treatments Susan's hair became exceptionally shiny and easy to manage. The chemotherapy seemed to give it life and sheen. She was pleased with its manageability. If the combination of drugs could take away her cancer and add zip to her hair, she could tolerate the nausea that gripped her stomach like a vice after each treatment.

So it was very distressing for Susan when she was in the shower a few days after her second treatment and her hair began to fall out in soft bundles. When I walked into her room in the hospital, she was sitting in her bed with a crestfallen look on her face. "Mom, you won't believe what happened," she said, choking back the tears. "It looks like I'm going to lose it after all."

She told of drying her hair and a patch as big as a silver dollar fell out in her hands. So the shiny, manageable hair was going. And it went fast. By the time we brought her home, it was so thin she had to begin wearing a scarf on her head.

As soon as she realized that the hair loss was mostly from the back of her head, she stopped lying flat on the pillow. Instead she would lie on her side, with her hands under her cheek to support her head. High hopes that this new position would slow the hair loss were dashed as the hair continued to come out in handfuls.

I asked her if I could go wig shopping for her. She replied with an emphatic "*No!*" I was afraid for her; afraid that she wasn't accepting her inevitable baldness. My hairdresser and friend, Maggie, suggested I purchase a wig and just leave it at the hospital. No need to force Susan to wear it; just have it there so she could try it if the mood struck.

Armed with information from Maggie about styles, types, and so forth, I went to the shopping center. On my next visit to Susan I brought with me a beautiful light-brown wig curled in the then-popular Dorothy Hamill style. But Susan was not enthusiastic. She refused to try it on. I put the wig back in its box, where it stayed for several days until her friend Liz coaxed her into trying it on.

"Come on, Susan," Liz teased, "why don't you just put it on for a minute and walk with me over to show Bonnie? Besides, how can you know for certain that you won't like it if you never even put it on!"

So Susan consented. In Bonnie's room next door, Susan stood looking in the mirror while Liz worked on her new head of hair. Without much to secure it, the wig slipped easily, and on the third brushstroke, it fell off Susan's slick scalp onto the floor. Susan leaned over, picked up the hair, and without a word she hurried back to the privacy of her room. The wig went back in the box where it stayed for several more weeks.

Bonnie and Susan had been growing closer and closer and were having long conversations about Susan's leukemia. Bonnie shared one of their talks with me. She said Susan had told her that she could accept death as the end of her leukemia, but she had so many things she wanted to do with her life that she wasn't about to throw in the towel without a fight. "And you, Shirley, you are a very brave person," Bonnie continued. "Just as brave as Susan. To have to face all this every day. I don't know how you do it!" she said, looking at me as if I were a saint.

I put my hands up. "Oh please don't say that, Bonnie! I'm not brave at all. Susan is the brave one, not me." I couldn't bear the thought of someone giving me a compliment like that. Bonnie didn't really know me. The real me went home every night and cried. The real me had a twisted knot in her stomach every day when she arrived at the hospital. Fear yes. Desperation yes. Grief yes. But bravery, no.

"But you always seem so *together*," Bonnie said.

"Sure," I said, choking on the lump in my throat.

"I'm trembling and falling apart on the inside, while I paste on a smile for Susan." I guess I had adopted a protective facade of my own.

After her second chemotherapy treatment, Dr. Sagone scheduled Susan for a second bone marrow test to see if the leukemia cells were still active. The test is given by inserting a long hollow needle into an area of active bone marrow in the hip. The marrow is drawn out through a syringe. Although the whole process is quite painful, it is the most accurate way to keep track of leukemic cells.

In a journal entry at that time Susan described leukemia as "a terrifying death shadow haunting me night and day. The notorious possessor of life creeps in and painfully takes over by poisoning my veins with his viper fangs. . . . It leaves me helpless to suffer with aggravating pain."

We held our breath as we waited for Dr. Sagone to tell us the results of the bone marrow test. We prayed that the chemotherapy had put a halt to the "death shadow."

5

HOME! BUT THE WEAK FALL AWAY

Remission. What a beautiful word! The chemotherapy was doing its job, and Susan's bone marrow test showed no increase in leukemic cells! When Dr. Sagone told us the news, Susan's face shone. A smile as big as Christmas spread across her face.

"Wow! It was all worth it. I've won!" she cried. The joy spread through us all, and I said a silent prayer of thanks.

Susan was feeling well and her spirits soared. She was anxious to go home. It took John and I two nights to carry the plants, cards, paints, paper, and flowers from her room. Susan wanted to say good-bye to all the people on her floor. So the morning of her dismissal she spent going in all directions saying good-bye to nurses, aides, orderlies, and other patients.

When Susan and I walked out to the car, we both

felt a sense of victory. Death was a remote possibility. Medicine, Susan's courage, and her faith had helped her win—at least the first round.

Our son Steven had made a big "Welcome Home" banner, and Windy, our dog, met us at the door with her tail wagging. She licked and whined all over Susan and followed her all over the house.

Our daughter Brenda was still at school when we got home, so Susan had a chance to decorate their room with notes. She spent more than an hour writing "This is ridiculous!" on small pieces of paper and stuffing them everywhere, teasing Brenda about her untidyness. Weeks later Brenda was still finding the notes in her bed, clothes, shoes, drawers, vanity, and picture frames.

After twenty-four days in the hospital, Susan was eager to resume her normal activities. She had high hopes of returning to classes during the spring quarter at Ohio State, but Dr. Sagone vetoed that idea. Although he promised her she would be strong enough to register for a few classes in the summer quarter, she was bitterly disappointed. Loving college, enjoying classes, she saw education as steps on a ladder that would help her reach her goal. The following is from an entry in Susan's journal:

> Those who have no interests, hobbies, goals, etc., to give meaning to their lives are merely existing. They are just here. They begin to deteriorate like a vegetable left to rot. Goals and interests give meaning to our lives, give us something to reach for, look for, grab onto, to keep going. Determination to accomplish these is really living. Even through all the discouragements and disappointments, life is worth the struggle. The rewards you receive will be well worth the effort.

Susan's strength and energy returned gradually that spring. She was anxious to attend church, but concerned about wearing a head-scarf. I casually recommended the wig but was careful to add, "or the scarf would be fine." It was the first Sunday in over two months that our children had attended church together. Steven was waiting downstairs for Brenda and Susan. Brenda came down and said Susan was almost ready. The minutes passed. "Come on Susan, this is *ridiculous*," Brenda called teasingly up the stairs.

When Susan appeared at the top of the stairs, we all caught our breath. Brenda's smile told us she had helped with the transformation. Susan had the wig on, the style was combed perfectly, and she was lovely. We all told her how nice she looked, and she accepted our compliments timidly.

Brenda told us later of the tears in Susan's eyes as they worked together to make her new head of hair look just right. Susan wasn't convinced of our sincerity, but she really lit up when one of the parishioners came up to her after the service and said, "What a beautiful haircut, Susan! Did you have it cut that way while you were in the hospital?"

Many other people commented that Sunday about how nice Susan looked with her new hairstyle. Little did they know that their words were a soothing salve to Susan's wounded pride. Putting on the wig became easy after that.

Soon after that day Susan went with me to University Hospital to visit my brother, Donnie, who was being treated there for chronic leukemia—a very different form from Susan's. Donnie's leukemia was a slow-moving type; he had been treated off and on for over ten years. His treatment procedures were vastly

23

different also; he never received chemotherapy intravenously, just pills. After our visit Susan was eager to show her wig to staff members on the floor and in the clinic. We passed a resident doctor in the hall, and he didn't even recognize her.

"Aren't you going to say hello?" Susan asked as he strolled by. He turned around, doing a double take.

"Susan?" he asked incredulously. "I'm sorry, I didn't recognize you all dressed up, and with your hair! You look terrific!"

Her ego was boosted another notch.

I never really got used to seeing Susan without hair. Her scalp was not shiny pink the way men's are when they are bald. It was grayish-white, and I continually fought the urge to look away.

Susan's wig was hot, and I knew the scarf was uncomfortable to wear at home; so I asked her to please not worry about how she looked around us. "After all, Susan," I joked one day, "You were born with only a little fuzz on that head of yours, so I already know what you look like without hair!"

After our discussion she seldom wore the scarf when only the two of us were alone in the house, but it was never farther away than her back pocket. If somebody rang the doorbell, she would quickly grab for the scarf and tie it securely over her head.

Dave and Susan had been dating steadily before she went into the hospital. It was at his suggestion that she went to the emergency room at University Hospital. He was a faithful visitor while she was hospitalized, running across campus from his dorm every night to check on her. After she was released from the hospital and home again, he visited a few times, but never stayed long for fear of tiring her. About the middle of March he called and said he needed to talk something over, but not on the phone.

He and Susan sat in the living room for a long time that night. John and I went to bed. About midnight we were awakened by a light tapping on our door.

Susan came into the room and sat on the edge of our bed. "You know what Dave asked me?" she said. "He wanted to know if I could guarantee him two years. Would I be alive two years from now?" Her voice trembled, and I put my hand on her arm.

"You know what I told him? I told him I could be hit by a car tomorrow and die right in the street; that life gives no guarantees."

Dave's visits became less frequent after that night. Because his family lived out of town, he went home for the summer months. Susan didn't hear from him again until Christmas, when he phoned. Perhaps their relationship would have ended whether Susan had leukemia or not, but she did take his rejection very hard. From that time on she had a fear of letting people know about her illness. "What if they can't handle it?" she would ask.

6

MAKING ADJUSTMENTS

Susan had said to me many times in the hospital, "I just hope I feel good enough to run again, Mom!" She loved exercise and missed very much the physical exertion of playing sports.

Susan was resting in her room one day while I sat reading the morning paper. A chill ran up my spine when I saw the death notice of her orthodontist's thirteen-year-old son. He had succumbed to leukemia after a two-year battle.

Susan came downstairs a few minutes later, and I knew I had to tell her. Our whole family had been wondering if Greg was any better. She sat quietly while reading the article. Suddenly she slapped the newspaper on the arm of the chair. "Let's go play tennis, Mom! Come on!" Before I had a chance to answer, she pushed a racket into my hands and was half-way out the door.

There is a tennis court in the schoolyard right behind our house; so in just a few minutes we could be there. The vincristine Susan was getting in her chemotherapy affected her agility; so sometimes her knees would buckle and down she would go. This happened on the way to the tennis court. One minute she was walking beside me; the next minute she was down on the ground. But skinning her hand and knee did not keep her from wanting to play.

We hit the ball back and forth until her scarf fell off. She grabbed it from the ground and glanced around to see if anyone had seen her. "Let's go home, Mom. I don't want to play anymore," she said. A little later I heard her upstairs, crying.

Susan had set out that day to prove something. After learning of Greg's death, she was more determined than ever to prove that her life hadn't changed, that she had come through her ordeal unscathed. Her test was a failure.

On April 16, 1978, Susan was readmitted to the University Hospital for spinal taps and the first of twelve radiation treatments. Leukemic cells have a tendency to hide in a person's cerebrospinal fluid. Anti-cancer medications that are carried through the bloodstream do not reach that area because the fluid in the spine does not mix well with blood. So radiation is administered to kill any cancer cells that might be hidden there.

Waste products are created when cancer cells are destroyed, and many patients experience nausea after radiation therapy. Susan was no exception. She was so sick during the second week of therapy that she carried a plastic bag with her at all times. After each treatment she lay in the back of our station wagon, sick to her stomach all the way home.

Susan then began to lose her hair again. This

28

time it was not as traumatic as before because the "peach fuzz" covering her scalp wasn't really much of a loss. Her only comment as she rubbed the top of her head, feeling the soft hair come off in her hands was, "Well, Mom, here we go again."

She remained reasonably well in remission that spring, and Dr. Sagone OK'd her class schedule for the summer quarter: Sculpture and Studio Art. He advised her to explain her condition to the professors. "In case any complications arise, they should be aware you are undergoing treatments at the clinic," he said.

Susan still had a difficult time saying the word *leukemia*. She was afraid to let strangers know she had it, afraid they would avoid her, or worse yet, be nice to her out of pity. It took all the courage she could muster to tell her professors; but she came home after the first day of class, bouncing in the door, declaring that she had met her challenge.

"They were super, Mom!" she exclaimed as she tossed her books on the kitchen table. Both professors were understanding, she said, and unlike people her own age, they did not stand with their mouths gaping open when she told them. There was no pity, just acceptance. Their attitude was a real boost to Susan's spirits. She felt "regular" as she completed assignments along with the other students in her classes.

A strange situation occurred that summer. Susan came home after each art class with a peculiar complaint. "Every time I walk into the art building, I get sick to my stomach. I have to run to the washroom and vomit before I can even go to class. It's ridiculous."

She told me how her nostrils felt dry and constricted, "just like when I'm given vincristine." It was a real puzzle to all of us. So Susan mentioned her symptoms to a nurse at the clinic the next time she went for a treatment.

Once Susan had described the symptoms, the nurse asked if there were any flowering plants outside the art building. When Susan said yes, the nurse answered, "I'll bet they're periwinkle plants. Do they have little blue flowers?" Yes again.

"Well, Susan, you'd better find another door to go in or hold your nostrils when you walk by those plants, because vincristine is made from the periwinkle plant. Evidently the scent from those flowers is enough to trigger your senses and induce nausea!" Susan rolled her eyes and laughed, "Even nature is against me!"

She was back in the hospital for a week in July when her blood pressure dropped drastically. The vincristine was the culprit that did it, so her medication was changed to another anti-cancer drug called 6-MP. Susan became nauseous after undergoing a spinal tap during her stay and was given an anti-nausea drug called compazine. Her body reacted violently to this drug.

The seizures started at four o'clock on Wednesday afternoon and lasted until late the next day. John and I were terrified as we watched Susan's back arch, her feet and legs draw up, and her eyes roll back in her head. After the seizure passed, she was completely exhausted. We could see the horror in her eyes as another seizure began. Every forty-five minutes for twenty-four hours her body convulsed into positions we had not thought humanly possible. Needless to say, that was her last dose of compazine.

Thursday afternoon, after the compazine was completely out of her system, Susan and I walked down the hall and out onto the patio. It was a bright clear day. Susan turned her face to the sun, sighed and said, "Oh this is such a beautiful day! I wonder if people appreciate the sun? I can feel its warmth clear through my body, clear through to my sore muscles!"

A gentle breeze blew around the corner of the building and Susan chuckled. She had attached "Old Faithful" to her IV pole, and the breeze made Woodstock look like he was flying. He bounced on his coil spring, his head and side feathers ruffled by the briskly moving air. Susan's muscles were so sore from the seizures, it hurt her to laugh. But laugh she did as she watched her funny friend flying across the patio.

Susan was home by Saturday and back in classes on Monday. Determined not to fall behind in her studies, she declared she would sit in class propped up in her seat if necessary.

That summer Joyce Bennett asked Susan to design a new logo for the Lioness Club. Susan was thrilled at the opportunity and worked diligently until she came up with a drawing of a baby lion with gentle eyes and a happy smile. The club members were pleased, and the picture still graces the club's official letterhead.

Susan's hard work in her art classes paid off. She finished the summer quarter with a B average.

7

SUSAN FIRST HEARS THE NEWS

During her first remission, Susan continued classes at Ohio State University. She wrote the following essay for a writing workshop:

The experience of an emergency room can be horrifying, but it can also be a lifesaver when you're in pain. When I went to the emergency room, it was a terrifying experience for me.

I had been in extreme pain for several months. My family doctor did not know what was wrong with me. I could not stand the pain any longer. I moved with much bone pain and with very little movement in every joint. My head ached like I had one whopper of a hangover. I decided to go to the emergency room at Ohio State University, after the big blizzard hit.

I got to the emergency room and the big double

doors opened before me. I moved slowly toward the desk. I asked to see a doctor. They needed personal information before I could be seated in the waiting room. The doctors examine you according to the nature of your condition.

Sitting in the waiting room can be an experience all by itself. There are many people moaning, groaning, crying, throwing up, and bleeding. The nurses are rushing around giving aid. All the moaning and groaning makes you feel like you're on death row. Finally, you get to go on the examining table, and the nurses leave you alone to stare at the ceiling or at the curtains around you. It seemed about an hour before the doctors came to see me. They kept poking my painfully tender body. They asked questions like: Why did you come here? Does this hurt? Why have you lost weight? Are you scared? Each doctor asked questions like these over and over. They seemed to want a confession from me. I felt like I had just committed a serious crime.

After all the x-rays and blood tests were finished, the waiting process continued. I felt like I was on trial, waiting for the hanging judge to give me my sentence. While I was waiting impatiently for the results, more injured and sick people kept coming in for treatment. You can imagine the kind of pain they're in. I couldn't help but feel sorry for them, even though I was in pain too. As I waited, I began to wonder if anyone had ever died on the table I was sitting on.

I'm sure glad these walls can't speak. I would hate to hear the stories they could tell. Just the thought of it sends shivers up and down my spine. Finally, after six hours of waiting, my "sentence" was given. this would be my doom for sure. I was to go into the hospital for more testing.

I could tell by the actions of the doctors and technicians that whatever I had was very serious. They stared at me as I was being wheeled out of the emergency room. They acted as though I had leprosy. I could tell they were uneasy, even though they tried to hide it. This made me very upset and I started to cry. I was in a strange place by myself with a mysterious ailment. My life seemed to have ended.

I called my family when I got to my room to tell them what had happened. The next day, when the testing was over, I was told I had leukemia.

It's been a year since my experience in the emergency room, and now I'm supposed to be "cured." I am very grateful for all those who helped me when I needed it. I know that without their help I would not be here today. Even though emergency rooms are terrifying, what would we do without them?

To have hope, you must have faith; to have faith, you must have courage; to have courage, you must have a will to live.

Susan Holdren

8

HOPES FOR A
BRIGHT FUTURE

Susan was still in remission in the fall of 1978 and feeling very much like her old self. Our spirits were soaring. We were nearing the one-year mark. The doctors had told us if she could hold her own for two years, "she would have it made." Halfway home and Susan looked great.

She attended a Lioness Club meeting with me in November. She had painted several pictures for the club's annual fund-raiser auction and was introduced in front of the group. Several people came up to me afterwards and told me what a beautiful daughter I had. It was hard for them to believe she had been so sick; her complexion was radiant, her eyes full of their old sparkle.

Susan had always been timid, especially in large groups of people. But months of illness had given her a new outlook. She was so grateful to be feeling healthy again, joy and enthusiasm flowed from her very being. She told me how great it was "to be free." She was in love with the world and everyone in it. The way she mingled with the members of the club and accepted their compliments on her appearance and her paintings was not the old shy Susan. This new Susan, who thought she had conquered the "terrifying death shadow," was confident, exuberant, and glad to be alive.

Dr. Sagone had OK'd a light class schedule for the fall and winter of 1978. Susan eagerly delved into sociology, art, and art history. She also worked part-time at a computer center authorization department answering the telephone, and she started dating a man named Mike.

In January Susan went sled riding with John, Steven, and two of Steven's friends. She loved the snow, but had to put on layers of warm clothing to protect herself from the cold temperatures. One of the side effects of the chemotherapy was lower body temperature; Susan was always cold, especially her feet. Before leaving the house that day, she caught a glimpse of herself in the full-length mirror. "My gosh, I look like the Loch Ness monster!" she laughed. Four pairs of socks, long-johns, two pairs of pants, sweater, shirt, blouse and coat, wool scarf, insulated boots, two pairs of gloves and a wool stocking cap pulled down over her scarf forming an oval around her happy face. And she was still cold!

It was during that winter that Susan really began to focus on what she wanted to do with her life. In high school she had a friend, Betsy Bachtel, who was deaf since she was three. Susan marveled at Betsy's accomplishments; she was a good student and a very talented athlete. Betsy was the star of the track team, and after graduation she competed in the World Deaf Olympics in Bucharest, Rumania.

Susan became preoccupied with deafness, bringing reams of material home from the library on the subject. Her professors at school suggested she visit a school for the deaf, observe the students at work, the teaching methods, and so forth. Since Susan demonstrated remarkable patience when working with little children at church, I suggested she visit the preschool classes at the Alexander Graham Bell School for the Deaf. She phoned the school and arranged for a visit.

I'll never forget the look on her face when she came bursting through the kitchen door after the first visit. She was breathless, her eyes sparkling, her cheeks aglow. "Mom! I know for sure what I want to do with my life! I want to teach art to deaf children!" She had a goal, a purpose, a pathway to channel her energies. A dream for the future. Henry David Thoreau said it best; "If you have built castles in the air, your work need not be lost, that is where they should be. Now put foundations under them." Susan was ready to begin building her foundations.

The following are Susan's own thoughts about her future as expressed in a paper for one of her classes at Ohio State:

> My life ten years from now will be everything I have ever wanted. I will be teaching deaf children and living in the wilderness as a nature painter.
>
> First of all, I see myself living in a homemade cabin of timber from the forest of the Black Hills in South Dakota, along with my companion, a golden retriever. Here I will be far away from hurried city life and hospitals. City life is too fast for me, and I become very nervous and unstrung. My

leukemia will be cured, and I won't have any more needles jabbing the tired veins of my body.

With the aid of a telephone, radio, and jeep, I will be able to come in contact with civilization when I have a need to, especially when loneliness manages to creep up on me when I am not looking.

I see myself as an art teacher at a local deaf school. I feel a kind of joy, love, and peace when I am around these children that I can't find anywhere else. I always feel happy and content after being with children. Also, I may be a Sunday School teacher at the nearest Methodist church and would like to have a class of children, elementary school age. I'm sure I'll be learning much from these children, as I hope they will from me.

In my spare time I hope to become a well-known painter of nature, since I will be living in the wilderness. There I will have firsthand experience. Also I want to learn to play the mandolin. It would be a new and different experience for me. It might even help me to become more creative in my work.

I plan to read many books on nature and philosophy to expand my knowledge of life and hopefully get to know myself better. I'm sure that ten years from now my life in the wilderness as a painter, teaching deaf children, and being with my golden retriever will make me happy and content for as long as I live.

Susan Holdren
English 110
Summer 1979

9

UP, DOWN, AND UP AGAIN

In December I gave Susan a body permanent; her hair was just long enough to wrap around the small rods. A long-time friend, Mark Stillings, gave her hair combs for Christmas and she was pleased to shed her scarf and wig.

After the last day of her winter quarter exams in March, Mike took Susan out to celebrate. John and I went to bed before they returned and were sound asleep when she slipped into our room. I was awakened by her hand on my arm.

"Mom, I hate to wake you, but I'm having that terrible bone pain again. I'm slipping back, Mom, I just know it," she cried softly. Her head was throbbing as it did before. I hoped my eyes did not reveal the terror I was fighting as I sat rubbing her arms, legs, back, and forehead.

She had dragged a promise out of us some months before to never, never have her taken to the hospital in the emergency squad. "They are dreadful and only for the dying," she said. We wanted to phone Dr. Sagone that night, but she insisted we wait until morning. The pain continued to increase, and Susan phoned the doctor at dawn. He told her to go right to the hospital.

Dr. Earl Metz was on duty that morning. Susan really liked him because he was always joking about her Woodstock collection. Dr. Eric Kraut was in the hall later that morning and gave us all a ray of hope, assuring me things weren't as bad as they appeared.

"We'll just have to start over, that's all. She's had a setback, but it's not the end of the world. Don't worry, we'll get her back in remission again." His positive attitude bolstered our spirits and enabled me to draw on a mysterious inner strength to encourage Susan to continue her battle against the "dragon who was poisoning her veins with his viper fangs."

As I was going into Susan's room that afternoon, Mike was just leaving. He looked pale and drawn, standing first on one foot and then on the other. After he left I asked Susan if Mike was OK.

"No, Mom, he isn't. He's not up to all this."

That was the last time Susan ever saw him. A journal entry after "Mike":

When I start to get interested in a guy, I feel hopeful. Even though I say to myself, "Don't be hurt again." At first when a guy starts to take an interest in me, I want to run. Maybe I'm afraid. But I always decide to take a chance. Then it seems that just as I start having strong feelings for him, he panics. I blame myself. But maybe all men are like that. Afraid of getting hurt, so they hurt first. Men and their egos!! How about mine?!

It was during this stay in the hospital that Susan began to grow close to other cancer patients. Susan Price, her roommate, was twenty-five, the first young leukemia patient our Susan had come in contact with. She had been a victim of Hodgkin's disease since she was fifteen, and the doctors had recently diagnosed leukemia. Something in me hated to see the girls become friends. What will it do to Susan if she has to watch a close friend *die* of her disease? My hope was to protect my daughter from more pain, but she didn't see it my way.

Susan Price was from Massillon, Ohio and didn't know a thing about Columbus. She had never been on a college campus before. So our Susan took it upon herself to show her around. When I came to visit one day, their room was empty. A nurse told me Dr. Metz had given them permission to stroll around the campus; so I sat in their room and waited. Pretty soon I heard laughter coming from down the hall. In they came, both looking flushed and happy. In between licks of their ice-cream cones, they told of their adventure. It was so good to hear Susan laughing and sharing with her new friend! I knew I couldn't stop her from caring about other patients; I knew I didn't want to.

Their laughter melted a hard place in me. I now view that period as a real turning point in Susan's illness—an opening of her heart, and mine. It was a subtle beginning of our finding a purpose.

Next we met Joanie. She was a tall redhead, only one year older than Susan. She had a faster-spreading leukemia. Those two also became good friends, with Susan walking every day down to Joanie's room to visit. I found myself being drawn into their relationship when Susan told me of Joanie's craving for licorice. I began to put pieces of red rope candy in my bag when I packed a snack for Susan each day.

And then came the young man, twenty-one years old. A nurse from the clinic, Nancy Hayes, told Susan what a difficult time he and his new wife were having trying to accept his Hodgkin's disease. The doctors wanted to start chemotherapy right away, and he and his wife were confused and bewildered. I couldn't believe my ears when Susan told me she had gone down the hall to talk with them about receiving chemo. She told them the good and bad aspects of treatment, wanting them to be aware of the realities. She came back all bubbly and proud of herself. What was happening to my *shy, retiring* daughter?

Dallas, the older man Susan had met the year before, was still in the hospital. He was in a depression, refusing chemotherapy and staying in his room. Apart from his own health problems, two of his best friends had recently died, and Dallas viewed life as anything but worthwhile. When Steve Smallsreed, the aid who was Susan's friend, told her about Dallas, she went straight down the hall to visit him.

Susan and Dallas had a long talk, and when it was over, Susan's spirits were down. "Mom, Dallas has lost his will to live. I tried talking to him about faith and about God, but I don't think I even dented that hard exterior of his." The next day Susan was scheduled for a blood transfusion. You can imagine her surprise and joy when she saw Dallas, whose room was in the opposite wing, quite a distance away, walking slowly toward her with the help of his three-legged cane and Steve Smallsreed. It was a very long walk for a man who hadn't been out of his hospital room for weeks.

"Honey, I just wanted to see how you were getting along. No need to be afraid of getting blood, you're gonna make it, so do whatever you have to do to stay well!" He shuffled back down the hall while Steve lingered for just a moment.

"I don't know what you said to that old fellow, Susan, but he's out of his room and has consented to start chemotherapy again!" Steve smiled broadly as he put his hand on Susan's shoulder.

Within two weeks Susan was back in remission and home again. Her beautiful curly hair started to fall out for the third time. Elsie Lockwood, a close friend of my mother, came to visit Susan that April. Elsie had leukemia and had lost her hair from chemo treatments also. "But look at it now," she said, "all curly and thick! I had to have a haircut after only nine months. Yours will be back again in no time, prettier than ever!" Susan didn't despair. She knew hair loss was a small price to pay for being one-up-again on leukemia.

Susan had signed up for art education, English, and psychology during the spring quarter but was forced to drop out because of her setback. She spent the spring attending confirmation classes at Maize Manor, mushroom hunting, drawing, doing needle-point, and getting to know herself. Here is a journal entry from April, 1979:

> I am letting my mind wander through the deep dark halls of my true self. My inner feelings are starting to emerge from the darkness within, to air in the consciousness of my mind, to know and change for the better. Then they will slowly be tucked away until the feelings swell within. For when they swell, they must slowly be released to ease the pressure of insanity. As my mind wanders through the maze of logic and reason, my feelings will alter and break, creating new thoughts and ideas like living cells multiplying and transform-ing. Thus, the new creation will be pondered and thought about. As ideas start to grow, these new creations will transform as they move through the maze of my consciousness, only to return once more to my subconscious mind. It's best to let my

thoughts run wild, for then I may get a better perspective of my true undaunted self. It's important for me to come to a real understanding of how I feel about myself, my life, and those around me, so that I may improve and readjust to my environment. I want to be the best I can be, in the short life I have. I want to help others to better their lives. It might help if I didn't judge myself so harshly.

It was Mother's Day when Susan suggested that we all go mushroom hunting. Brenda and Steven had made other plans, so John, Susan, and I headed for West Liberty where we had scoured the woods in previous years for the expensive supermarket delicacy. I was afraid for Susan when she wandered off alone that day. She was falling so much, and I guess I wanted to be nearby to help her up. I kept my motherly instincts to myself, and we all went in different directions each with a sack for the harvest.

It wasn't long before I heard Susan cry out. My insides churned and I called, "I'm coming!" and I ran as fast as I could. John had also heard her, and we barely escaped collision when we met along the path. When we reached Susan, we saw a very excited young woman, calling out because she had found a whole bed of succulent mushrooms. Her cry had been one of joy not pain.

We picked the mushrooms, then, and all rested on a log before heading back to the car. Susan was in her glory surrounded by the big trees. She commented dreamily as she leaned against the damp log, "Oh, it's so peaceful here, so nice." She pointed out different wildflowers and birds. She was happy, peaceful, and in remission.

What a Mother's Day gift!

10

BARGAIN WITH GOD

It was a busy summer for Susan. She was back in school at the university taking freshman composition and art. Every two weeks she returned to the clinic for spinal taps. After a few days of nausea and tiredness following these treatments, she was back at her easel or desk.

On the days she was scheduled for spinal taps, I would drive her to the campus and wait outside the English building so I could go with her to the clinic. It was always so peaceful while I waited on a bench, sometimes reading, sometimes working on my quilt. The sun was shining warmly on my face, birds were singing as they flew overhead, and squirrels were scampering across the lawn.

Chimes would ring, and soon a group of students would pour out the double doors. Susan's blue-hankied-head would be right in the middle; she would be joking and laughing with her friends. Watching her among her peers made me understand just how much Susan needed this involvement. Listening to them discuss papers they had to write, exchanging reference sources and authors, seeing how caught up in learning and *becoming* Susan was, I realized, perhaps for the first time, just how important getting an education was to her.

My heart ached as fear crept into my mind. I bargained with God; "Susan was too valuable to die! She would become so important to the deaf children who needed her, right God? Too many of us need her . . ." My inner self was screaming while I calmly walked with Susan across campus to the University Hospital and the painful spinal tap.

One of the papers Susan had to write that quarter was, ironically, about death. Here are her thoughts on death as written in that paper:

> Death is the ending of life. The stoppage of breath, the loss of all bodily movement, being unable to have relationships with others, all these separate the dead from the world of the living. There are several concepts of death which can be described as: physical death, freedom, a dream, departure of the spirit, and a journey.
>
> Physical death is when the heart stops and the blood no longer circulates to bring fresh oxygen to the body cells. Not all cells of the body die at once. The death of some cells actually begins even before we are born. For example, certain cells decay and are replaced with new cell structures. This process continues throughout our entire lives. This type of process happens to a snake when he is molting. The snake's outer layer begins to wither, and the dried skin begins to peel off. In its place is a new layer of skin. The molting process of the snake continues until he ceases to exist.

Death also frees a person from the limitations of the body. For example, a handicapped person is confined to a wheelchair and is unable to move his arms or legs. His death will then free him from his bodily bondage.

We might also picture death as being the departure of the spirit from the body. We can suppose that the sleep of death is like the dreams we have when we are asleep. One evening we may fall asleep and venture into a state of dream. In our dream we are running through an open field of flowers. We decide to stop and pick a handful of yellow daisies. But when we wake up, we find ourselves snug in bed and discover that we were not really out picking daisies. So, like death, our bodies had remained in bed, our souls had gone to pick the flowers.

We might think of death as being a mysterious journey into a world from which no one has ever returned, except our Lord Jesus. We can imagine we are inexperienced travelers with a trustworthy tour guide. We then begin our grand adventure through a misty tropical rain forest. We have traveled all day, brushing against the dense underbrush on either side of an old worn path. In a small clearing we camp for the night. The next morning we find our guide has left us. We then break camp and begin to fight our way up the worn path. Later we find our tour guide has gone ahead to prepare a place for us in the world beyond. There he will greet us as we stumble in.

Our Christian life can be compared to the journey through the rain forest. Jesus is with us as we travel through life on the path that has been traveled many times before. But as we come to the close of our natural life, Jesus goes ahead of us to prepare a place for us in heaven. Once we reach our destination, Jesus will welcome us with open arms. Our journey will then end.

We can also compare death to apples in an orchard. When the apple is fully ripe, it is then picked from the tree that gave it life and is placed in a bushel basket. Thus a human life, full of years, is picked from the tree of life and is placed in a basket of eternal life.

Death is the departure from the world of the living. A true separation from all living things.

» » »

After a spinal tap, the patient is supposed to lie still for at least an hour to avoid the headache that often follows this procedure. Susan would usually take a book to read during this time. But one day she felt particularly restless and wanted to draw on the large blackboard hanging in the clinic room. She asked me to wheel her cart over to the board so she could draw some cartoons of Woodstock. One pictured him sitting snugly in his nest with a caption, "I only come here for the punch . . ." (Chemo patients receive punch or candy to remove the metallic taste in their mouths after treatments.)

Another sketch showed Woodstock with an IV pole and a bag with a wine glass at the end of the tube. The caption read, "And you thought it was only medicine?!"

Drawing was such a release for Susan. The joy she received from Charles Schulz's fuzzy-topped bird brightened her life and the lives of others she came in contact with. She drew many pictures and cartoons for fellow patients, and her room became the talk of the hospital. With Woodstock hanging from her IV pole, and with her collection of Snoopy and Woodstock cards on the wall and the door, there was always cheer. Even the times she spent in isolation were brightened by Woodstock, who wore a miniature mask and gown that I had made for him.

Our family took several weekend camping trips in the summer of 1979. Susan played hard, as if she were making up for lost time. At the campgrounds there were lots of people, all ages, and there was always activity. Susan went bike riding, played volleyball, horseshoes, and softball. In the evenings she was exhausted and went to bed early in the camper.

Susan still did not have enough hair to make a difference; the headscarf was always on. One day she was swinging on a rope over a creek, and she fell in. Her wet scarf clung tight to her head. It was a hot day, so she bravely took off the wet cloth and stuck it in her hip pocket. A little boy about five years old came up to her, pulled on her pant leg, and asked, "Why do you cut your hair so short?"

While my stomach tightened, his mother simply explained to him about Susan's illness and the medication that made her hair fall out. He looked up at Susan, not the least bit embarrassed, said "Oh," then turned to the other children standing around the picnic table, said, "Let's go play!" and he ran off toward the creek.

"That kid is neat," was Susan's comment as she watched him skip away.

11

DETERMINED TO WIN

Susan was delving deep at this time. She was changing, making discoveries about herself, about her relationship to God and to the world around her.

Here is a journal entry she made in the summer
of 1979:

> There are several things I wish to do before I die.
> I want to make love to someone who really loves
> me. I want to leave good seeds behind that will
> grow and benefit others. I know that some of those
> seeds I leave behind will be trampled and strangled
> or left unattended. Others will start to grow, but
> will later be choked by weeds and die. But I hope
> some of them will fall on good soil and grow to
> their fullest and be rich to benefit many.
>
> I want to show myself that I can do anything.
> I want to be somebody that maybe not everyone
> will know, but those whom I have touched will
> remember. If I can't do great things, I want to do

small things great. I want to be able to prove this to myself, satisfy myself in knowing that I have helped others. I have felt inferior in my early life. I dreamed a lot to hide from reality. In my dreams I could be anybody and do anything. I could make things happen the way I wanted. Now I want to make some of these things happen the way I wanted them to happen. Now I want to make some of those dreams come true. I don't want to feel inferior anymore.

I always felt inferior, like I was never good for anyone. That's one reason I never ran around with friends too often. I was so shy and inward. Afraid to show my true feelings for fear of being laughed at. That's why I liked being alone. I was afraid to get too close to anyone for fear of getting hurt. I didn't like myself much. Now I am finding out that I'm not inferior. I am a good person who always seems to be taken advantage of and trampled on.

I have come to know I must believe in myself. I do surprise myself at times. I know I can do anything I want to if I set my mind to it. Don't ask me why I feel this way, I just do. It is something I can't explain, even to myself. I hope with God's guidance I will achieve what I am here for. I want to be an art teacher in a deaf school. I want to get married and have children. I can remember my Grandma Holdren telling me about Aunt Ginny's three wishes she wanted to have fulfilled before she died. Ginny was my favorite aunt; she died of leukemia in 1969. She was about twenty-three at the time. When she died her three wishes had been fulfilled. She was a vocal music teacher, she was married to Uncle DeWitt, and she had a daughter Heidi Rae. I was ten years-old at the time. I feel as though I'm following in her footsteps. I found out I had leukemia when I was eighteen.

I want to teach, get married, and have children, just like Ginny did. I have a good chance of beating this horrible, terrifying death shadow that haunts many people such as myself. Aunt Ginny didn't have a chance to fight this notorious killer. I do, and I'm going to put up a pretty darn good fight. If this death shadow is going to take full control of my body, it's going to have to put up a real good fight.

I have asked Jesus to take away all my problems, sorrows, pain, burdens, and I want him to do what he will with my life. I know that I have leukemia for a reason. But I don't know what the reason is yet. I am sure I will learn what the purpose is as time goes on. I must have tolerance and patience to wait it out. I really want to teach those deaf kids, and I hope that this is what God wants me to do. Those kids bring a special joy and love to my heart that many people don't give me. It always brightens my day and adds cheer to my heart just to be with them.

In August Brenda, Susan, and I went to see the stage musical *Shenandoah* with Ed Ames at Veterans Memorial. We enjoyed the evening very much, and Susan didn't tell us until the next morning how miserable she had felt. Her jaw began swelling and her tooth was really causing her pain. Dr. Sagone recommended she have it taken care of immediately and gave her penicillin to take for three days before the dentist could work on it.

"Why didn't you tell me you weren't feeling well?" I asked.

"Because I wanted to be with you and Brenda, and besides, I didn't want to ruin your evening by getting sick and leaving."

She was determined to win.

12

"LET SUSAN BE DIFFERENT . . ."

In late August, 1979, Dr. Sagone told Susan he had seen a few leukemic cells after her last bone marrow test. "Not many, but we have to halt their growth or they'll get away from us, Susan," he had said.

"Can I finish my summer classes?" she asked hopefully.

"How many weeks left in the summer quarter?" His hand was cupped over his mouth, so we knew he was considering her request.

"One, and then exams. I have to finish, Dr. Sagone; I've worked too hard to miss those exams!"

"Well, we can't get you a bed right away, so I guess you'll have time to finish your classes." She clapped her hands and he chuckled—a rare expression for serious Dr. Sagone. Susan then asked about the fall quarter.

"No way, Susan, you'll be in the hospital for at least one week a month for ten months," he said. Her face fell; her tears told of her disappointment.

"Well, maybe it has to be this way for awhile, but don't think I'm going to give up on school entirely!"

Even though classes were ruled out, Susan found other ways to enhance her knowledge. Phyllis Hall, a pharm tech, began bringing Susan books on sign language and even helped her learn some basic signs. She could count to thirty, sign *yes, no, love,* and her name. Phyllis had two roommates who were deaf and were students at Ohio State; so she was able to tell Susan their recommendations on the latest books for learning signs and learning about deafness.

Susan had no idea that the summer quarter would end her college career. She was too sick in the following months to attend classes. In spite of pain, hospital stays, clinic visits, nausea, and overall weakness, she finished Ohio State with a 3.35 accumulative average.

Since the onset of her leukemia, Susan had kept notes about her chemotherapy, dates in and out of the hospital, room numbers, and so forth. They were written on pieces of scrap paper, napkins, or whatever else was available. In September she began keeping a more accurate and neater record on a small pocket calendar. A typical daily entry might look like this: "chemo-allop., ara-C, bone scan, wgt. 114, blood test, bleeding gums, bone pain." It was evident from her handwriting whether she was having a good or a bad day. Bad days were signified by shaky lines and lopsided letters, more like a four-year-old's first attempt at making letters.

Susan was back in the hospital the first week in September and immediately inquired about Dallas.

Steve Smallsreed came into her room to say hello. "Is Dallas still here? How's he doing?" Susan asked.

Steve's tall, thin frame sagged; his expression told of Dallas's fate before he spoke. "The chemo wasn't working, Susan. Dallas wanted to go home and spend time with his grandchildren. He died in early April," Steve explained solemnly.

"But he promised me! He said he would fight!"

"You got him as far as he could go, Susan. He *did* try. Dallas lived a long life," I said, mustering the most reassuring tone that I could.

Oh how it pained me to see the shadow of grief and fear pass over Susan's face! "The chemo wasn't working." Those words cut like a knife. But that was Dallas. He had lost his battle because he laid down his arms too soon. Susan's life would be different. *Yes, Susan's life would be different.* Of course there would be ups and downs, but we could handle those.

The first stay in the hospital that fall lasted two weeks, and Susan received eight doses of chemotherapy. Dr. Sagone dismissed her then, but after two days at home we noticed splotches of red just below her skin. They soon began to appear all over her body. Having been warned of this danger sign, we knew that her platelets had dropped to a very low level. We made our way back to the emergency room where we waited a long time for a room. I sat on a little black stool beside Susan's bed and we talked.

"You know, Mom, this is a lot better than the first time I came to the emergency room. You are with me, I know I have leukemia, and this is a new emergency room [new addition]. These walls don't have as many stories to tell," Susan said. When she was finally assigned a room, we were happy to see it was large, with a tremendous view of the city. We were grateful for the view that day, because the next morning Susan was put in isolation because of her very low white blood cell count.

That was a difficult time for Susan, because she couldn't leave her room. No visiting with other patients, no roaming the halls. While she was in isolation, Grandma and Grandpa Holdren gave her a Woodstock that climbed up and down on a string. I made an isolation cap, mask, and gown for him, and he brightened the room as he dangled from Susan's IV pole. Rev. Gene Wells came to visit her there, and Susan had to guess who it was under all the sanitary paraphernalia!

It was at this time that I became better acquainted with Joanie. Since Susan couldn't take Joanie her licorice, I began going into Joanie's room to drop it off.

Three of Susan's high school friends, Diane Haines, Renee Davis, and Barb Serkerek, contacted me at this time with an idea. It was very difficult for Susan to change her gowns when she was taking chemotherapy because of the IV pole. These treatments would last for a week, and by that time Susan was feeling bad enough without having to lie in a soiled gown. These girls, with the help of Barb's mother, Betty, bought her four gowns and suggested that I cut the shoulders and put velcro fasteners down both arms so it would be easy to change gowns. It worked beautifully. Susan and I were both so grateful for their thoughtfulness and caring.

The hospital stay lasted for two weeks that time, and Susan's hair began to fall out for the fourth time.

John and I celebrated our twenty-first wedding anniversary the weekend that Susan was released. Neither one of us felt up to celebrating, but the kids insisted. "You haven't been out alone together in ages!" they argued. "Go! Eat! Have a nice leisurely dinner!" They practically pushed us out the door.

Before the leukemia, pranks and fun were an integral part of our household, via Susan. She was the self-appointed agent who continually strove to lighten the drudge of day-to-day living. Her father was her favorite victim. He often found popcorn stuffed in the toes of his shoes, or his socks were tied in knots in the top drawer of the dresser. Susan never lost that childlike spirit of silly fun, and our home was a brighter place because of her liveliness.

John decided to take our annual Christmas card picture at the campgrounds. On Saturday, October 13, 1979, he and Steven drove to Bellefontaine to prepare for the picture. Susan was nauseous and worn out, so I drove up later with her and with Brenda. We had been taking these pictures every year since the children were small.

As we all sat posed around the campfire, I felt time stop for an instant. Surrounded by the people I loved most, I fought back tears of happiness and fear. I was happy that we were all together, able to be a part of this traditional picture; but I was fearful of time snatching the serenity of the moment.

Susan sat quietly on an old log, while Brenda and Steven laughed at Windy racing around in the dry leaves. How many years I had taken health, happiness, and normalcy for granted! How close, confined and very small my world had been before Susan's leukemia.

My inner self cried for *more time, more of the past, more normal days.* John set the timer, ran back to join us by the campfire, and we all smiled into the camera lens.

13

INTERNAL PEACE

On a Monday in the middle of October, Susan was back in the hospital with severe shoulder and back pain. She objected when they wanted to put her in Means Hall. She was well aware that that was where patients were moved when chemotherapy had failed to arrest cancer growth. Means Hall meant experimental drugs. Means Hall was one step away from the end of the line.

The nurses explained that experimental drugs were not the reason for Susan's placement. It was simply a matter of space. There were no rooms available on her regular floor, so Means Hall was taking the overflow for a few days. This calmed her. The nurses kept their word, and in a week Susan was back to the main hospital.

On the day she moved from Means Hall to 10 East, a man about Susan's age, with longish dark-blonde curly hair came into her room. "Hi, Susan, I'm

Bob Holomuzki. A friend of Steve Smallsreed. I'm a registered nurse on this service, and Steve told me to take extra-special care of you. He'll be by after he gets off work to check on us—to see if you're doing OK and to see if I'm being good to you." He laughed, and from that day until Susan's death Bob became a very special friend, just like Steve. They were both in and out of her room often, supplying humor when Susan needed to laugh and kindness when she needed a friend.

Nellie Davis was Susan's roommate on 10 East. She was a leukemia patient in her sixties and almost immediately she felt a grandmotherly affection for Susan, Brenda, and Steven. Her hair was about an inch long and stuck straight up all over her head.

I came to visit one day and brought Susan's baby barrette. We were laughing as we tried to get the tiny barrette clasped to a few spindly hairs on Susan's head. Our laughter offended Nellie.

"Why are you so rude to us, Shirley? You are such a nice person, but yet you stand there and make fun of us without hair!" Nellie exclaimed from her bed.

"I didn't mean to be rude, Nellie. We're laughing *with* you, not *at* you," I answered.

"Yea, Nellie," Susan chimed in. "I used to be hurt by comments, too; but you know, once I let myself laugh about it, I felt a whole lot better. There's not a whole lot we can do to change the looks of these stubbles," she continued, rubbing her hand over her scalp, "so we may as well smile and accept the facts."

Nellie's attitude changed after that, and she often talked about Susan's spirit and her will to make the best of a bad situation.

It was homecoming that week, an exciting time on campus. Susan was feeling down because she couldn't participate in any of the festivities. I brought her a pair of binoculars and her spirits lifted somewhat as she watched the homecoming game and parade from her room overlooking the stadium.

On October 27, Susan's calendar entry read: "OSU Homecoming. Blood Test. Allop. wgt. 114½." On Halloween Eve she was given two units of packed red cells and ten units of platelets. The nurses pre-medicated her, thankfully, because they had a very difficult time trying to find a good vein.

Holidays were always special events in our family, so we couldn't let Halloween slide by without a celebration—even if it had to be in the hospital. I made a mask for Woodstock; we all carved pumpkins and had paper cups full of apple cider. Joanie was ambling up and down the halls with a sheet over her shoulders "trick or treating" in the patients' rooms. "I'm the ghost of 1980," she declared. Fear tightened around my heart when I heard her say those words, but I tried to dismiss any painful thoughts that Halloween night.

Dick Reed, a friend of ours and a Sunday School teacher from our church, came in dressed like a bird. I couldn't tell whether he was trying to look like Woodstock or just a feathered friend, but Susan giggled when she saw him. Dick and his wife Donna were faithful visitors and card-senders the entire two years of Susan's illness.

Susan, Brenda, and Steven had always joked over which one of them would give me the most gray hair. When I walked into Susan's room one day, she handed me a piece of paper. On it she had written the following Bible verse: "Long life is the reward of the righteous; gray hair is the glorious crown." (Proverbs 16:31)

She was in good spirits that day, teasing me about the sprinkle of gray that was beginning to appear in my light-brown hair. "See, Mom, the more gray, the better you become!" She chuckled, then a thoughtful expression came across her face, "But I wish my being sick wasn't so hard on you."

"Don't be silly," I answered quickly. "It isn't only you, you know. I'm beginning to worry already about your baby brother getting his driver's license next year!"

"Well, anyway, I think you're lucky, Mom. At least you have hair to turn gray!" she said, rubbing her scalp.

"Susan, have you ever heard the saying, 'God made some peoples' heads perfect, the others he covered with hair?' " I said.

"Oh Mom, come on!" and we continued our light bantering. We had learned a long time ago how good it felt when laughter dispelled grief.

Susan soon began working on Christmas decorations. Working with her hands was a great release. She was much happier when she was "creating." I lost track of the red felt Santa booties she made and sold that year. I do remember that she kept me busy running back and forth to the craft shop for supplies.

During visiting hours we worked together. Because her fingers and palms were a little numb—a side effect of the chemotherapy—it was difficult for her to use the scissors; so I helped cut out the patterns. As word of her "craft shop" spread around the floor, orders began coming in from nurses, other patients, and even visitors to the floor. Susan was delighted, feeling useful, and she didn't have time to grieve over missing classes at the university.

It was during this stay in the hospital that we met Dorothy Robbins. She was a delightful woman, a high school guidance counselor in her early sixties who became very close to both Joanie and Susan. Dorothy and Susan exchanged cards and letters when their paths didn't cross in the hospital. Each was very interested in the other's condition. Dorothy enjoyed doing needlework as Susan did, and they were always commenting on each other's work.

Susan made a Santa bootie for Dorothy. John and I went with her to Dorothy's room to deliver it. "Hey, Dorothy! I brought you an early Christmas present to brighten the days ahead!" Susan said enthusiastically. Dorothy was unable to appreciate the gift because she was suffering terribly from a penicillin reaction.

"Susan, I don't think I'll even be here for Christmas," she answered, just above a whisper. Susan became visibly upset and dashed out of the room. Something inside of me said, "Ah-hah! See what happens when you grow close to other patients?" And for just a moment I wished we had never met Dorothy; we surely didn't need the pain of losing her.

Joanie's room was our next stop; but she had a fever, so we left the bootie with her mother. How it hurt to see those friends in such misery! But it did make us very thankful for Susan's reprieve, however temporary.

On November 8 Susan was able to come home for the day. When she went upstairs to her room, she began yelling, "Mom! You won't believe this room! My bed is so full of Brenda's junk I can't even lie down!" I went up to help unpile Brenda's things, and Susan was steaming. But how good to see spirit! There had been times since her last remission when I became worried about Susan's apathy. I knew how difficult it was for her to be enthusiastic when physically she felt so bad. I rationalized all this, telling myself that time would heal her wounded spirit. So deep inside I was pleased with this display of anger, taking it as a sign of a coming remission.

On November 9 Susan's calendar entry was: "L-asparginase, vincristine, pred., allop., blood test, wgt. 116½."

When I walked into her room shortly before Thanksgiving, Susan was sitting up in bed reading her Bible. "Mom, *I know why God gave me pain!*" Her voice sounded so positive, so happy. Her cheeks glowed. I sat in the chair near her bed, searching frantically inside my head for a cheerful response.

"You know how I have always been so reserved, scared of strangers, afraid to talk to people? Look how I've changed!" Her hands were folded across her Bible, her eyes were the softest blue I'd ever seen. "He is using me as a tool to help others. You didn't know I was talking to new chemo patients, did you, Mom?"

I shook my head, feeling my throat fill with emotion. She continued, "The nurses have been letting me know when a new patient comes in for chemo, and I go down to talk with them. You know, sort of help them overcome their fears. There's no way I could have done something like that two years ago! God has given me the courage to help others and it's OK, Mom. Really!"

I hugged her then, and for the first time since she was a little girl she said, "I love you, Mom." Tears were streaming down both our faces. Oh, I had seen how Susan was changing, but how I wished it were me that God had chosen! How I wished I could be at peace with her plight the way she apparently was.

"Thanks for helping me, Mom; thanks for coming every day!" The sound of her tearful voice was muffled as she clung tightly to my neck.

Susan had found her peace, her reason for suffering all the pain and agony that a disease like leukemia brings. She was so full of love and acceptance. Oh, she just couldn't leave us!

"Me?" I said. "Why are you thanking me? I should be thanking you, Susan, for allowing me to stay with you."

14

BLESSINGS OF CHRISTMAS

On Thanksgiving Susan was allowed to come home for the day. Brenda was ready this time. She had strung an adding machine tape down the middle of their room. "My side, your side," she explained. "See, I'm getting better about neatness, or at least more thoughtful!" They shared a laugh and the sound of their happy voices coming from the bedroom was most welcome to me. My Thanksgiving Day prayer contained a thank you to God for my daughters' laughter.

Later that day I heard a racket coming from their room. Peeking inside the door, I saw the girls having a pillow fight, playing like they used to when they were small. I leaned against the wall outside their door, sighed, and wiped away a tear from my cheek.

Susan had gotten to know Marge and Ginny,

check-out girls at the Big Bear supermarket where we always shopped. For years I have done my shopping early in the morning to avoid the long lines, and Susan was always up and ready to go with me. These women knew Susan was sick, but it was hard for them to realize just *how* sick, because she was always so chipper when she was in the store. Susan would visit with them as she helped to bag the groceries.

Marge and Ginny sent Susan a basket of fruit with a large can of chow mein noodles on top. Susan laughed, "How did they know I was craving those noodles?"

Her roommate was fascinated. "In a city the size of Columbus, Ohio you get to know the *check-out ladies*?" she asked.

I thought about that, and realized how lucky we were. It was that kind of caring, from old friends, new friends, and neighbors that helped us hold up through our ordeal. People reaching out, caring, with their cards, flowers, candy and other gifts. I was learning how very much my life was changing, how my attitude was changing—almost as much as Susan's.

Susan was getting cabin fever, and she wanted to take a walk outside one day in early November. We went to a nearby park and sat on a bench feeding the squirrels. It was a beautiful fall day; brilliant foliage, crisp air, and the sun was high in a pale blue sky. Joanie's father was walking in the park also and stopped to say hello. Susan visited with him and told him about her ex-roommate, Lois, who was put on experimental drugs.

"Oh, I didn't know. How is she responding?" Mr. Schneider asked.

"I really don't know," she said quickly. Too quickly.

Lois had died. I had stopped in to see her one

day before visiting Susan, and a nurse told me she was gone. Susan was afraid to ask about Lois, afraid of what she would have to hear. She didn't talk about Lois again until after Thanksgiving.

"Mom, Lois died didn't she?" she finally asked. Her only comment when I told her yes, was "Oh."

First Dallas, then Susan Price, now Lois. "Who would be next?" I cried inwardly.

Joanie was next. She died right after Thanksgiving. Susan was at home, helping with the dishes when she heard me gasp, "Oh no!" as I read Joanie's death notice in the paper.

"What is it, Mom?" she asked anxiously. John came in from the family room. When we told Susan, giant tears rolled down her cheeks. "At least her pain is over. Can we stop by the tenth floor tomorrow and get her address so I can send her family a card?"

We did, and we ran into Joanie's brother at the desk. Susan told him she was sorry. They stood, it seemed for the longest time, just looking at one another with tears in their eyes. How I ached watching them and wondered what thoughts were going through their young minds.

In December John, Brenda, Steven, and I received a card in the mail which read:

Dear Mom, Dad, Brenda, Steven, and Windy,
    I just wanted to thank all of you for the gifts, time, and efforts during and after the hospital trips. I want you to know how much I appreciate everything you have done for me. It really helps me to know you are behind me all the way.
    Sorry it hasn't been easy for you all.

Thanks again.

Lots of Love,

Susan

73

On December 8 Susan had to be hospitalized again; this time for four days. Her gums were sore and bled easily. Even brushing her teeth ever so gently caused bleeding, and she began to use a plastic stick with a foam tip furnished by the hospital to clean her teeth.

Susan was in the clinic on December 14 for a chemo treatment when Dr. Sagone stopped in to see her. He told her of a strategy. A new medication was to be given to her which required a hospital stay of one week a month for eight to ten months.

"Dr. Sagone, what does this mean? Am I in another remission?" she asked anxiously. He put his hand on her shoulder. Susan's expression fell, and she fully expected the worst. He chuckled. "Yes, Susan, you are in remission!"

What a Christmas gift! We bounced out of the clinic, flew straight home, and decorated our tree. Susan was on an emotional high. She sent her own Christmas cards (with Woodstock on the front) and scurried around the house helping me decorate. She even decorated the basement where John had his darkroom. Our normal procedure was not to put gifts under the tree until Christmas Eve, but Susan couldn't wait. She had all her gifts bought, wrapped, and carefully arranged under the tree a week before Christmas. On Christmas Eve we entertained my side of the family. Susan visited and laughed with her aunts, uncles, and cousins and played with the little ones. When the relatives came, they brought with them a large basket of small, individually wrapped gifts for Susan to take back to the hospital. They wanted to make her Christmas last a few more weeks by having a gift for her to open each day.

At one point during the evening, Susan had disappeared. Looking upstairs, I found her resting on her bed. "I just got a little tired; I'll be down in a little while," she said. After a short rest, she was back downstairs enjoying what was to be her last Christmas with her family.

On Christmas Day John's side of the family had us over to West Liberty. Again Susan enjoyed the celebration. The relatives commented, "She's different. So bubbly and playful." She had reason to be. Remission; a period of grace.

Susan was exhausted after the two-day celebration. The next day she spent in bed, regrouping her strength and getting ready for her December 28 return to the hospital and the beginning of her maintenance program.

Susan spent New Years Eve sick to her stomach and vomiting. We spent the next day watching Ohio State play in the Rose Bowl. I made a sign out of brown paper towels which read, "Go Bucks"; and I blew up balloons and attached them to a piece of cardboard. Susan was to break a balloon with a syringe each time the Buckeyes made a touchdown. Ohio State lost 17-16.

As I sat in the chair next to Susan's bed, putting tiny stitches in my quilt, I wondered what 1980 would bring. Would Susan remain in remission? One of her favorite Bible verses read: "When hope is crushed, the heart is crushed; but a wish come true fills you with joy."—Proverbs 13:12. I was praying for a wish to come true.

Knowing that after each relapse a remission is more difficult to come by, I went to God asking for the improbable.

15

SLIPPING

On New Year's Day Susan began keeping a diary. Writing in her little black book, recording what happened each day seemed to be a great release for her. Here are some excerpts from her diary:

Tuesday, January 1: In the hospital. Ohio State lost 17-16. Taking chemo. Had headache and got sick. Had to have IV changed to right arm, left arm too sore. Can hardly bend it. Went to see Nellie, my former roommate.

Wednesday, January 2: IV infiltrated and they had to change it back to left hand (it is still sore). I have only two more bags of chemo to go. Nellie to go home. Hope to get home Friday. I saw Laura Shay today. Ordered a sub from Pizza City to celebrate the coming year, since I didn't feel like it on Monday or Tuesday. Still have headache.

Thursday, January 3: Nurses had to find a new

IV site. I had two IV's in one arm with chemo running and two units of blood. Mom and Dad got
me a Woodstock in his nest that is motorized.
Nancy Hayes from the clinic brought me Woodstock bandages. Started working on the needle-
point owl Aunt Betty, Uncle Alvin, Beth and Brent
gave me. I get to go home tomorrow.

Susan was ready for her trip home the morning
of January 4. Her suitcase was packed and standing
by the door. She was dressed and sitting on the side
of the bed when Dr. Mark Segal came into her room.

"Susan, your platelets are real low. I don't think
it's a good idea for you to go home," he said. But seeing her crestfallen expression and her packed suit-
cases, he softened. "But I see you're all ready." He
looked at me and asked how the driving was in the
snow. After I assured him that the roads were not
hazardous, he turned to Susan. "Susan, you know the
signs; if anything goes wrong, call here right away."
I saw her body relax and felt my own relief as I released my breath. We needed to be together as a family again; Susan needed to be home among familiar
things.

Friday, January 4: Snowing today! Came home.
Platelets low; sure hope they don't call me back
to the hospital on Monday. So nice to be out of
that hospital room. Took a nice long nap and used
the new comforter Aunt Olive and Uncle Don gave
me for Christmas. Should be able to get a good
night's sleep tonight.

Saturday, January 5: Had a great night's sleep.
Headache almost gone. Felt good enough to go
shopping. Aunt Louise stopped by with Janice.
Snowed all day.

Monday, January 7: Cold out! Blood test. Had to wait over an hour to get test results and see if I needed antibiotics. My counts were 1,800; what a relief! Worked on art dictionary, owl needlepoint, Nancy Hayes's Siamese cat. Started exercises. Still have headache.

Wednesday, January 9: Another day. Haven't had to get up in the middle of the night as often as I used to. Mom finally went to the doctor. They put her on medication. If it doesn't help, she'll have to go in for testing. I'll take Laura Shay one of my large Woodstocks. Hope it brightens her day.

Thursday, January 10: Went to doctor today. Got up feeling stiff and tired. I've got to go on a diet! All the weight I've gained on this prednisone is around my middle.

Saturday, January 12: Slept late again. I go into the hospital on January 27: Wrote thank-you notes. Worked on Mom's quilt and started my book on essays. Sure hope I'm not getting a cold; that's all I need.

Monday, January 14: Laid in bed until almost noon. Did exercises, studied a little, worked on Mom's quilt. Mrs. George, our neighbor, came over to see me. I called Denise Kern about her wedding. It is this Saturday evening. Don't think that I should go; it feels like a cold coming on. Sure hope not. Got a card from Aunt Sheryl, Annette, and Wayne.

Wednesday, January 16: Went to the clinic this morning. Got a chest x-ray to see if I had an upper respiratory infection causing my cough and running nose. It was clear. Slept most of the day.

Thursday, January 17: Got dressed early this morning to get groceries with Mom. Slept most of the day, since I don't feel well. One of these days

I want to go to the library and call the Ohio State School for the Deaf about more info.

Friday, January 18: Got up to the ringing of the phone. It was Barb Serkerek. Then Mrs. Bownas, my neighbor, wanted me to come over. The two of us went to the Northern Lights Library, and I got several books on deafness. Felt better today. Got a note from Laura Shay.

Monday, January 21: Slept in late again. Don't feel like doing much. Taking notes from library on deafness and some of the causes. Trying to find a picture of Pigpen to draw for Dr. Segal.

Tuesday, January 22: Slept late. I felt as if someone had just hit me up the side of the head. Found a good picture of Pigpen. Got the picture drawn and ready to frame. Taking more notes on deafness. Drew Mom a cartoon about the quilter, "If I don't finish it, it will finish me!" Aunt Louise, Lou, and Mike came.

Thursday, January 24: Had clinic appointment. Went with Mom to Big Bear before clinic. It was snowing pretty hard, so many patients didn't show up. We got right in. I had a bone marrow, so I can start chemo Sunday. Blood count higher than ever. Thank God!

The doctors told us that Susan was slipping. The bone marrow aspiration showed leukemic cells were again growing and beginning to spread. I had learned over the past two years to take one day at a time. Susan barely flinched when we told her the news. I knew how depressed she had been before, but she always fought her way back to the top. She would do it again.

Saturday, January 26: Slept as long as I dare. Dad took pictures of the paintings I did last summer.

Getting packed for tommorrow. Did a bunch of odds and ends before I go in. Sure hope it goes fast.

Sunday, January 27: Slept in. (Hospital) Had three physicals, blood tests, EKG. Aunt Olive, Uncle Don, Sarah and Dave Kearfott stopped by. Ralph and Alice Stacy too.

Monday, January 28: Talked to Tom from Lima, Ohio. He goes home tomorrow! Was told today that they have found some leukemia cells in my bone marrow.

16

LOSSES AND GAINS

Susan was overwhelmed by the kindness expressed by her friends and family. Grandpa and Grandma Holdren as well as numerous cousins, aunts, and uncles kept John supplied with gifts for Susan. There was not a night between the end of January and the ninth of March that he came home from West Liberty, where he worked and where his family lived, empty-handed. They made sure he had something to take to the hospital every night. Even his salesman and secretaries jumped on the bandwagon. The gifts ranged from stick-people drawings by her little cousins, to fruit, flowers, and cards—all gentle reminders of their love and concern.

Wednesday, January 30: Woke up with a nagging backache. Sure hope it is nothing serious. Bob and Marie Moore stopped by. Rev. Gene Wells stopped in. Still waiting for my chemo to come in the mail. With my luck, it will get lost. Grandma and Grandpa sent me a hopping, wind-up Woodstock.

Thursday, January 31: I had to have three blood tests and a 24 hr. urine test today. It snowed last night. Dr. Segal stopped by yesterday. Says he likes the Pigpen I drew for him. My blood count was up to 5,000 yesterday.

Friday, February 1: Today is two years leukemia. My chemo came in. Went to take pulmonary test today (lungs). They had to try three times to get an IV in. Mom stayed all day with me. Things went OK, but I was queasy all night. Laura Shay gave me one of her sorority pictures; they were real good.

Sunday, February 3: Feeling a little better today. Stopped to see Laura Shay. Aunt Janet called.

Monday, February 4: Slept on and off last night. Had nosebleed. Rev. Wells came. So did Steve Smallsreed. Bob Holomuzki came in for a free valentine kiss. Aunt Olive and Uncle Don also stopped by.

Tuesday, February 5: Got blood drawn today. Didn't sleep much last night. Started chemo today. Called advisor yesterday, so I may be able to go for the spring quarter! Talked to my roommate, Opal. She is going back to a nursing home to die, even though she is in partial remission.

Susan considered Opal her only failure. "Mom, Opal is the first person who wouldn't listen to me! She has given up her fight and is going home to die!" she said to me that evening. "I just can't let her do that!"

"Susan, there are some people who have to do things their own way. Opal has made up her mind and is evidently at peace with her decision. You have done your best," I said. But Susan was not satisfied; she just could not understand how anyone could refuse chemotherapy—she knew it was the only chance for even the slightest hope of survival.

> *Thursday, February 7:* Had blood test early. Feeling a tightness, heaviness in my chest. Tender bones and stiff leg joints, dry mouth. Should get chemo today. Laura Shay is not doing so well. She is in no pain, though, and is alert. Mrs. Shay gave me the number to call Dick Maxwell at the Physically Impaired to help me get classes like he did for Laura. Mr. and Mrs. George brought me a flowering succulent. Aunt Louise and Kent, Mrs. Glassburn, Everett Lockwood, and Jean Steva came.

Susan was keeping tabs on her friend, Laura. On February 7 she asked if I would help her walk down to Laura's room. We ran into Barb Conley, the pharm tech, on the way, and Susan stopped to visit for a moment. Laura's mother was standing out in the hall and she pulled me aside while Susan was talking. Mrs. Shay said it was only a matter of time for Laura— she was very close to death.

"Try to keep Susan out of Laura's room. Seeing Laura this way will be very difficult for her," Mrs. Shay continued, her voice was quivering.

I was engulfed in Mrs. Shay's grief and didn't notice that Susan had walked into Laura's room. When I looked up, a pale and drawn Susan was coming toward me. Without speaking to anyone, she made her way down the hall alone. I fell in step beside her, she took my hand, and we made it back to her room before she started to cry. As I helped her into bed, she asked, "Mom, this is Laura's last day isn't it?"

Laura and Susan had grown close during the past year and a half. They talked about their classes at

O.S.U., compared notes on their shared disease, and discussed their Snoopy and Woodstock collections. It wasn't fair that Susan had to witness her friend's death. What would it do to her to watch another close friend succumb to leukemia?

"Yes Susan," I answered hesitantly.

"I knew it. Oh why, Mom? *Why does God want us so early?* You know I held her hand just now, and I told her I'd see her again someday."

I couldn't respond to her question. Dallas, Laura, Joanie, Susan Price, Lois; they were falling like dominoes. *But not Susan. She was going to make it.* I was still denying fate.

> *Friday, February 8:* Didn't sleep much last night. Got chemo yesterday and they had to stick me four times. Then they had to take out the hepburn well because it backed up last night. Barb Conley brought me a small box of stones. I got up today, but had to sit back down because I was blacking out. I think it is the chemo. Said I might lose my hair for the fifth time. Laura Shay died last night. Got a call from Dick Maxwell, will call back later in the week. Social service worker and Jeri the pharm tech came by. Got fruit from Grandpa and Grandma.

On Sunday, February 10, Susan was allowed to come home for the day. She asked for her favorite meal: ham, scalloped potatoes, and green beans. John's parents came over, and we had a very pleasant family dinner. Evening came and Susan dreaded going back to the hospital. She walked all over the house, saying good-bye to all the familiar rooms. I was in her bedroom helping to gather items she wanted to take with her. She sat on her bed, glanced around the room, and said, "You know, it's as if I've moved out of this hospital into an apartment of my own. Only it's different. I can't take everything with me."

Just before John took Susan out to the car, her eyes swept the living room. Windy was whining for attention at Susan's feet. She bent over and rubbed Windy's ears before retreating to the car.

As I watched Susan from the back seat on the drive back to the hospital, I wondered what she was really thinking. Why was she viewing everything in sweeping glances as if she wanted to fix everything in her memory? I know now that Susan sensed she would never go home again. But that night we couldn't talk to each other about her approaching death.

I helped her up to her room while John stayed in the car. Olive Witherow was her new roommate. "Well at last I get to meet Susan!" a tall slender woman in her early forties said with a warm smile. "I've heard all about you from the nurses. They said you were young and the most popular patient around here!"

Susan smiled and we were both moved by Olive's warmth and friendliness. "I was beginning to wonder if you were coming back, but I figured you wouldn't go away and leave the room all decorated with Woodstock's picture plastered everywhere!"

So Susan had gained a new friend. I looked up at her window as we pulled out of the parking lot. I wondered if she would ever make it home again. I would not allow myself to think negatively.

Sunday, February 10: Got to go home for the day. Really stuffed myself. Got my income tax forms. Library books and O.S.U. information taken care of. Dick Maxwell should be calling about this spring. Beautiful day at home; couldn't ask for anything better.

17

FACING THE TRUTH

Susan's hair had begun to fall out for the fifth and last time. She was still looking forward to attending classes. After contacting Dick Maxwell, coordinator of the Office for the Physically Impaired at Ohio State, she was really enthusiastic. (The program coordinates academic and physical support services for university students having special needs due to visual or physical impairment.)

She learned of the Bureau of Vocational Rehabilitation and phoned that office to inquire about help with her tuition and books. Thrilled and relieved to learn that she qualified for full tuition because of her "disease of the blood," she eagerly looked forward to classes. "I'll be a teacher yet!" she declared. "It will be much easier, Mom, with priority scheduling, career planning advice, and even transportation!" That evening I left a happy, hopeful young woman, absorbed in thoughts of pursuing her career.

Monday, February 11: Rev. Wells stopped by. Filled out valentine's cards. Met Diana Elchert from across the hall and her roommate Tammy. Told them all about chemo. Told them it wasn't all that bad.

Tuesday, February 12: Feeling great today. Had chemo yesterday with no problems. Got some letters written, valentines, and old thank-you notes. Had to pack up all my stuff since we will be moving to the eleventh floor while tenth floor is closed for remodeling. Hate to move. Barb Conley called, we talked a long time. Steve Smallsreed and Bob Holomuzki are bringing up a pizza tonight. Can't wait!

Wednesday, February 13: We made our move very easily this morning. It took time to unpack and put up all my cards. I had another chemo treatment; good so far. Jeri, the pharm tech, came by. Steve S. could not make it tonight, but Bob H. did. We had a medium pizza with everything on it. Bob brought me a large valentine!

Thursday, February 14: Valentine's Day. Got a lot of gifts. Flowers from the Lioness Club. Steve S. and Barb C. stopped by. Jeri called. Olive went home. Asked if Diana Elchert could be my new roommate. Talked to Dick Maxwell. Brenda called. Passed out valentine's cards to everyone. Received some more drawings from Karen, Aaron, and Joy to put on my wall.

Friday, February 15: Had a very busy day. Gave Mittie a valentine. Pat Stidham too. Mittie got to meet Dad. He stayed with me this afternoon while Mom went to the doctor. Had a bone marrow biopsy. Asperit went fine, but biopsy they had to do twice. Bob made a date to hold my hand while it was being done. (Pretty nice!) Got my chemo today. Had to start a new IV site. Barb Conley phoned.

The results of her bone marrow biopsy were not encouraging. "The chemo has stopped working," Dr. Sagone told me. "We've done all we can for Susan. All we have left are the experimental drugs."

So it was said at last. My heart felt the blow of a sledge hammer. After all the months of taking two steps forward and one step back, I had to face the fact that Susan had taken her last step forward. Feeling very old and tired, I wound my way slowly through the halls and back to Susan's room.

I was surprisingly calm. If a person can feel grief and relief at the same time, I know that I did. At least now it was out in the open; no more grasping at straws and wild dreams. Mittie, the nurses' aide who had befriended my whole family with her gentle, caring ways, was walking towards me in the hall.

"Shirley, are you all right?" she asked, taking my arm.

"Susan isn't going to make it after all, Mittie. She's losing ground," I said. The next thing I knew she had pulled me from the hall, through a door, and into the privacy of an empty shower stall. There we clung together and cried. I knew my family could not make it through this hell alone, but I was too numb to turn even to God for help. Dear Mittie had come to lead me in prayer. We stood there together in the solitude of a damp shower stall and prayed. Mittie asked for strength for Susan and for all of us to endure the coming weeks, while I prayed for strength to face Susan with the news.

When our prayers were finished, a poem by Helen Steiner Rice came to my mind. It had always been a favorite of mine, and that day I drew solace from the words the author had crafted so skillfully:

When I must leave you for a little while
Please do not grieve and shed wild tears

And hug your sorrow to you through the years
But start out bravely with a gallant smile;
Live on and do all things the same,
Feed not your loneliness on empty days,
But fill each waking hour in useful ways,
Reach out your hand in comfort and cheer
And I in turn will comfort you and hold you near;
And never, never be afraid to die,
For I am waiting for you in the sky!

Perhaps the poem was *His* answer. I was some-how able to enter Susan's room. She was sitting on her bed, her pale face was blank. Seeing me, she reached out her arms, drew me down beside her, and began to cry. Racking sobs. I learned the meaning of devastation that day as I held my dying woman-child, feeling my insides shatter and splinter with pain and torment.

"Mom, the chemo is not working. They want me to go on experimental drugs. I don't know what to do!

My tortured heart was somehow still beating. Not right. *Why can't it be me instead of my Susan?* "Susan, you know I would trade places with you if I could."

"Oh I know, Mom," she answered, drying her eyes, "I know."

Susan's roommate, Diana, witnessed this shar-ing of grief. She was packing her belongings to go home. "Susan! Where is the courage you tried to give the rest of us? Don't you have any left for yourself?"

Susan finished wiping her eyes, blew her nose, and that was the last time I saw her break down. She had less than three weeks to live.

Saturday, February 16: Was awake most of the night. Diana gets to go home. Doctors told me chemo is not working. Sent in my course selec-tion for spring quarter. Hope I can go. Think the marrow looks like it did last November. They aren't sure what drugs to use next. I feel great. Met a girl named Sheri from Warren, Ohio. She is in for her first chemo, even though she has had Hodgkin's disease for fifteen years. She has two boys. No roommate tonight. Started writing what I want when I die. Phil Hall, Stephanie Bacon, Connie Meade, Beth Peden, and a man named Keith had pizza with me.

18

WHAT TO DO IF
AND WHEN . . .

Susan's written requests:

All I request is a memorial service, and a small stone marker stating my name and date information. I would like a few flowers at the memorial service. The rest of the money that would have been spent on flowers, open casket, etc., be given in my name to leukemia research. (To be buried with family.)

Request about life support machines: If at any time I must be placed on a life support machine in order to prolong my life, when there is no other hope for recovery (even after a few weeks to a month or more) from conditions such as irreversible coma, and/or when my brain is dead or barely functioning, when only my body parts are being kept alive by machine, when I am just existing (no signs of movement, not knowing anyone, not being able to care for myself, etc.) I wish to be taken off the life support system and be allowed to wait for my "natural" death.

Terminal illness: I will permit doctors of leukemia/cancer research to use me, if needed, to try experimental drugs in order that I might be able to help someone else in the event there is absolutely no hope of my own recovery. I wish nothing to be given to induce my death. Only pain medication be given (by my request) in order for me to wait for my "natural" death.

Body parts I wish to donate: Eyes: any or all parts of my eyes to be used in helping restore another's vision. Ears: any or all parts of my ears to be used in helping restore another's hearing. Glasses/contacts: to be given to someone for reuse. Liver: may be given to anyone in need of a transplant in order to remain alive. Kidneys: may be given to anyone who is in need of a transplant in order to remain alive.

Monday, February 18: I will be starting a new chemotherapy from England called DCF. Used only in four other hospitals in the United States. Ten other people have started this new drug. Sounds like it works. Will be taken off prednisone and vincristine. I will be moving to Means Hall on 5 East to start treatment. Tammy, Diana's roommate, died last night. She was my age and just married nine months ago. After this chemo there is one more. And there is nothing else they can do for me.

Tuesday, February 19: Had a rough night's sleep. Lots of bone pain, and I guess I'm keyed up. Mittie Ray called and read me a Bible verse. Robbie Moseley also talked to me, along with Mary and some other nurses. Had a bone marrow. Rev. Wells came. IV started last night, it went well. Steve stopped, had a small pizza. Jeri stopped by. Joyce Bennett called.

The move to Means Hall was difficult. The concept of giving up, giving in, I could not accept. But somehow we managed, with Steven's help, to pack all of Susan's things and make this one last *move*. Bob Holomuzki accompanied us. I was still hoping Susan would be the exception, and that the experimental drugs would bring her into another remission . . .

Wednesday, February 20: I slept great last night. No pain. IV is fine. Gave urine specimen to young girl for experiment. God has lifted my worries, anxieties, tension, burdens. Got chemo around 6 P.M. Dad and Mom spent the day with me. About 9:30 I had sever side pain and lower back muscle cramps, shortness of breath and bone pain. Called Mom. She spent the rest of the night here.

Thursday, February 21: I am in so much pain I can hardly stand it. Nothing helps ease it. Went through all kinds of tests: blood, urine, lung scan, chest x-rays. Mom and Dad stayed with me all day. Finally they gave me morphine. It took the pain away. Ellen Madden came. All the gang from 11 Center stopped in with food. Can't believe how nice everyone has been to me. I'm so sore. Been getting blood and platelets.

Ellen Madden, Susan's friend from high school, had remained a faithful friend and visitor. I called Ellen to tell her Susan was failing, and she came right away. They held hands for a long while that day without much conversation. The bond the girls had always felt for one another went beyond words and a thread of love connected them that last visit.

Susan's room was at the end of a very quiet wing. We heard a commotion in the hall the evening of February 21. There were voices, footsteps, and then singing: "For she's a jolly good fellow!" About fifteen nurses came trooping into Susan's room carrying big platters of food. They finished their melody, "for nobody can deny," as Susan lay thunderstruck.

The room was alive with nurses. They were sitting on Susan's bed, leaning against the walls, sitting in chairs and standing in the doorway. Connie Meade leaned over my chair and grabbed my hand. "This is for you too, Shirley," she said. "We're with you all the way." I was so taken back by this lavish display of concern and generosity that I couldn't speak.

"What did I ever do to deserve all this?" Susan asked, smiling broadly in spite of her mouth sores. "I guess if all of you are fighting for me, I can't give up, can I?" The room was then in tears.

Friday, February 22: I feel so sore today. Can't believe this pain. Bob, Steve, and I wanted to get a pizza tonight, but I didn't feel up to it. Sure hope this is over soon! The doctor's can't believe this new chemo has worked! That's why I am having such pain. It is working! Patty Dunn started a guest list for me. Nancy Featheringhan gave me a Snoopy decoration for St. Patrick's Day. Nancy is the only one I will let take my blood.

Saturday, February 23: Can't hardly walk now, I am so weak and sore. Fluid restrictions. All events may not be in right order, but I'm trying to remember everything. My arms are all bruised and I have two good IV's. Thank God. Rev. Wells stopped by.

Sunday, February 24: Finally about to say "I Love You" to family without getting so emotional. Feeling stronger today. Mom came early to give me a bath. She is so great, just hope I'll be able to do the same one day. The drugs have been making me talk in my sleep, and I have been having rough nightmares. Brenda and Steven came up. Steven gave me a 50-cent piece for good luck. Ellen Madden and her dad stopped by. Aunt Wanda and Uncle Sam came with Grandma and Grandpa. Barb stopped after work today. Olive and Uncle Don. Dr. Metz stopped in.

When Brenda and Steven visited Susan on Sunday, she became very upset when it was time for them to leave. Steven handed her the 50-cent piece. She hugged him tight around the neck, saying, "I love you, little brother." And Brenda she hugged the same, "I love you, Brenda." She wanted to watch them drive out of the parking lot, so I helped her up in bed. She waved out the glass as they pulled away. That was the last time she would see Brenda and Steven.

Monday, February 25: I will be getting a bone marrow today. Found out the DCF didn't work. Don't know what to try next. I've been having fevers. Had chest x-ray and had to take potassium. Uck! It hurts to breathe. You should see all the black, blue, yellow, and green bruises! Even my rear end. Trouble sleeping.

When I came out of Susan's room that evening, an intern asked me how I felt about life support machines. "Would you want us to connect Susan to one when the time comes? The disease has already killed her, Shirley; it would just be keeping her alive."

Susan and I had not talked about life support machines. I did not find her writings on that topic until *after* her death. I cried all the way home that night after telling the intern to allow her death to come naturally. Did I do the right thing? My answer came when I found the paper stating that she wanted to die a natural death.

Susan began hallucinating. She said she saw Mary floating in a boat, and then it capsized. "Did they save her in time?" I asked.

"Oh yes, she was fine."

She also saw people standing around talking, but she couldn't tell who they were or what they were talking about. And her cousin Bruce was writing her a long letter; she could see him at a desk. Although she remained faithful to her journal entries, some were barely readable because of her blurred vision and constant pain.

Tuesday, February 26: Had more blood drawn. Chest x-ray and lung scan. Pneumonia in right lung. Put me on bactrium. Started oxygen. Easier to breathe. Aching pains. Can't get comfortable. Still don't know about chemo. Not sleepy.

Wednesday, February 27: Blood test, EKG. Started me on prednisone 6MP, methotrexate, and vincristine. Potassium. Still on oxygen. I have to take almost thirty pills a day. Had platelets. No appetite. Lot of pain, but it stopped. Barb Conley, Bob, Jeri, Rev. Wells, Bob Moore, Molly Morgan came by. Susan Henry sent a fun book for me.

Thursday, February 28: Diana, my old roommate, came in Tuesday. Don't feel like doing much. Still on fluid restrictions. Making me moody. Got grouchy with Dr. Metz. I asked him if he just came by to play with my Woodstocks. He told me no. I was so rude to him.

Friday, February 29: Leap Year! Miserable because of medicine. Bob, Steve, Barb, Polly Griffith, Mary Harden, Molly, Mrs. Hayes, Rev. Wells,

Aunt Martha, Uncle Bob, Ralph and Alice Stacy.
Got a call from Jean Steva. Devotion book from
Mildred Jones. Barb Conley gave me a back rub.
Wgt. 117. On oxygen.

Saturday, March 1: Can't believe it's March! Still
miserable because of prednisone and all the pills.
Jeri stopped by. Aunt Olive and Uncle Don came
and made supper for the family. Aunt Janet and
Uncle Richard, Cherly and Todd came. Chest x-ray,
white blood cells and whole blood. Wgt. 115.

While I was visiting one afternoon, there was a
Snoopy special on television. Susan laid in her bed
and watched Woodstock cavort across the screen, his
little cheeks puffing in and out while he whistled. She
laughed. "Oh Mom, I love that little bird so!" Laughter
was something I had not heard from Susan in weeks.

19

THE BATTLE IS OVER

Monday, March 3: Don't feel like doing much. Can't seem to get comfortable. Still can't eat. Losing weight. Left side ache. Mouth sores getting worse. Oxygen. Muscles quivering so I can't sew or write very well. Eyes blur after reading. Chest x-ray. IV. Bactrium, potassium, unit of white cells. Wgt. 113.

Tuesday, March 4: Horrible mouth sores. They say my lungs are clear. Don't feel like eating. Mom got me some baby food. Bob, Steve, and Rev. Wells came by. Grandpa and Grandma brought me a Woodstock Christmas ornament. White cells and oxygen. Sat up in chair to watch TV. Walked a bit.

Wednesday, March 5: Feeling better today. Been walking and every muscle is sore. Mouth sores. Watched TV, kept dozing off. More white cells. Ginny Clark and Margie Stackpole (from Big Bear) stopped in. Connie and Mrs. Stillings also.

Thursday, March 6: Slept a little better. Muscles so sore, tense and shaky. My eyes start to blur after awhile. Mouth is so sore. Might have yeast in my urine. Got a new roommate, Dorothy. Chest x-ray. Bob, Dick and Donna Reed came. One unit of white cells, blood test and oxygen.

Friday, March 7: Slept on and off. Having fever of 103. Makes me feel lousy. Got sick at breakfast. Nancy Hayes and her mom came. Grandpa and Grandma sent a fruit basket, so did Aunt Wanda and Uncle Sam. White cells, bag of multi-vitamins, prednisone, IV.

Saturday, March 8: Stuffed Woodstock from Bob and Marie Moore. Blood test. Chest x-ray, fever of 103-104 with cooling blanket. White cells. Dick and Donna Reed came. Aunt Louise and Janice came by. Chris Baumann gave me some suckers so it might help my throat. A funny: "a thermometer registering 104 while lying in a drawer; it's in the drawer with a hundred and four."

Dick and Donna Reed had stayed close to Susan the entire twenty-four months. They were Sunday School teachers from our church, and the three of them had gotten to be very good friends. Many times, just as we were leaving the hospital to go home, the Reeds would be coming. Susan was so delighted to see them, it made our leaving much easier. On their last visit, Donna left Susan a Helen Steiner Rice book. We read her several verses from it just before she died.

Last Entry

Sunday, March 9: Fever. Blood test. EKG. Private nurse. Steve and Bob came.

A resident doctor phoned at 11 A.M. on March 9 and told us to come to the hospital right away. Susan was slipping fast. I prayed all the way. "Oh God, please keep her alive until we get there!"

Susan was having a difficult time when we arrived. Her breathing was labored; her throat full of mucus. She was choking when we walked into the room. After a nurse suctioned fluid from her throat, she was more comfortable. Steve was in the room. We had met Bob out in the hall. It was so good to feel their support; they had remained so faithful throughout Susan's illness.

Susan's complexion was gray, her face was puffy from all the steroids she had received in the past months. She asked us to please read from her Bible to take her mind off what was about to happen. We read the 23rd Psalm, plus other favorite passages she had underlined in red, selections from her Daily Devotions book, and selections from *Loving Promises* by Helen Steiner Rice.

At 3:30 Barb Conley, the pharm tech from 7 Center, stopped by and read from a nature book and more of Helen Steiner Rice. When she finished, Susan asked Barb to clean her fingernails. She was awake but still laboring with her breathing. She asked me if I had brought my quilt.

"Oh Mom, I would love to watch you work on it. Everything has always seemed OK when you're hunched over that quilt." Her voice, for the moment, sounded stronger.

John left for home to bring back the quilt, and Carolyn, my dearest friend, came to read more to Susan. When she walked into the room, Susan asked, "Shouldn't you be home with your family, Carolyn? It's Sunday, you know; but I do thank you for coming!"

Somehow I felt we were actors in a drama: Susan, the protagonist, sitting up in her bed watching intently as I ran tiny stitches in and out of a calico star, Carolyn sitting in a green vinyl chair reading Susan's favorite scripture passages aloud, and John standing beside Susan's bed, cradling her thin hand.

People walking by the room and seeing our drama probably saw peace. *But my daughter was dying.* She was readying herself for her soul's journey to a new life. Slowly I was comprehending the reality of her approaching death.

Susan stopped Carolyn after she read a prayer. "Stop reading for a minute. I want to give my testimony to God." She closed her eyes and visited silently with our God. Carolyn read for a few more minutes until Susan said, "OK, you can stop now, I am at peace."

"Mom, could you help me bathe?" The nurse and I together cleansed Susan's worn, bruised body. She had about an inch of hair on her head, and she wanted it shampooed.

Susan then asked for a coke and an orange. She had not eaten anything by mouth for two weeks, and her sore, infected throat thirsted passionately for something cold and wet. John went to the cafeteria for a large coke brimming with ice and was given an orange from the nurses' station. When the coke cup was empty, we fed Susan the orange, little bits at a time.

Her feet were very dry and scaly. She asked if she could soak them in warm water. We helped her to a chair where she sat for half an hour wiggling her toes in a pan of soothing water.

She sighed, "Oh-h you can't know how good this feels." Settled back in her bed, holding tight to Woodstock, Susan talked of her love for the Black

106

Hills. "I wish I could go there again." John brightened. "Well, as soon as Dr. Sagone gives us the OK, we'll take you back!"

The false promise of his words hit me like a wrecking ball. Pain shot through my body, not leaving an inch untouched. Susan wouldn't make it to the Black Hills again; she would be dead in a matter of hours. Denying death would not make it go away.

Thoughts of the past two years swirled in my head. I had been fortunate enough to share closely with Susan. I had really gotten to know my quiet, inward, artistic child. We had laughed, cried, talked, embraced. We shared a closeness many parents never experience with their children. And I was grateful.

Suddenly Susan bolted upright in her bed. "Oh, I feel so high, so strange! What do kids see in taking drugs?" she cried. Her pupils were enormously dilated. "I don't want to close my eyes!"

Nurses appeared and asked us to leave the room. I knew this was the end; her struggle was almost over. In a small room down the hall where support groups for cancer patients held their meetings, I saw a book on the table, *Make Today Count.* We had done just that. Quietly sharing Susan's last hours: feeding, batheing, talking, and comforting. In a few minutes a resident came in. "I don't have to tell you what happened?"

"No, we know she's gone."

John and I hugged each other. "We lost, didn't we?" I said quietly to John. I asked to see Susan. Walking back into her room, seeing my half-finished quilt draped over a chair, her Woodstock pictures taped on the wall, her Bible open on the table, and Woodstock lying beside her bed, I said to myself, "So this is the quiet of death." My heart felt raw and bleeding, the pain was indescribable as I looked at

Susan. No more needles, no more tests, no more courage, no more tears, no more sharing. Her death expression was serene.

"I love you Susan." I kissed her and told her I would see her again someday. Turning around, I saw a young woman standing in the room. She was crying. I didn't know her and wondered if Susan had touched her life in some way. I couldn't ask. Feeling the sting of grief, I said good-bye to my first-born. It was so unlike the joy I felt when I greeted that fuzzy-headed birthday baby twenty years before.

EPILOGUE

Slowly, taking two steps forward and one step back, our family is adjusting to the gap in our lives. Evidence of Susan's studying her Bible in an effort to accept Christ as early as eleven years old has helped ease our pain. In a Bible she received in the sixth grade there were many underlined verses; most of them referred to accepting His will. In the end Susan was at peace with God, leukemia, her family, and herself. What more could life bring?

The Bible Susan took back and forth to the hospital was heavily marked; more evidence of Susan's diligent studies. Ecclesiastes 7:3 she had underlined in red: "Sorrow is better than laughter; it may sadden your face, but it sharpens your understanding." Reading that verse after her death, I suddenly realized the changes her illness and death had wrought in me. The whole experience had given me a clearer insight into human pain and suffering. Life would never seem simple again.

The organist played "Bridge Over Troubled Water" at Susan's funeral. As I sat listening to the song, it dawned on me how very many wonderful people had served as our "bridge" over the past twenty-five months. How could we ever show or tell all those beautiful people just how much their cards, flowers, phone calls, gifts, food, blood donations, love and concern had meant to us? Old friends, new friends, our family, doctors, nurses, aides, and technicians—so many had helped buoy our strength during those dark times.

A mere thank-you sounds so trite when it comes to showing gratitude to people like Ruth Stumph, our neighbor, who began bringing food to our house during Susan's last days; she also sought blood donors for her. To Bob, Pete, and Bill who frequently offered their blood to help Susan in her battle, a thank-you seemed stilted; but we hope they know their love and concern will never be forgotten.

Our other friends, Mark, Connie, Bill, and Jo-anne, sang *Now I belong to Jesus* at the service. Listening to those words brought us a renewed sense of acceptance. Yes, Susan is with Jesus; and Yes, I must let go.

Susan was a fighter. She was determined to win her battle with leukemia, complete her education, and become an art teacher for deaf children. Here are some excerpts from a paper she wrote for a class at Ohio State after her first remission. Rev. Wells read these words at Susan's funeral.

> I thought that it was the end of the world when my doctor told me that I had acute leukemia. He was glad that I came seeking help when I did. I only had one month to live without any medical treatments. I was in a state of shock. The only

question I asked was, "How did I get it?" He had no answer. I was dying, and no one had listened to me. I lost all hope until my doctor told me that I had a good chance to destroy this killer disease. With a series of drugs called chemotherapy I could live a normal life.

Deep within me a new surge of courage and hope appeared. This time it was a courage so strong that I withstood the endless attacks of withdrawal and sickness that was deathly. I had a good chance of recovering, and I was determined to beat this terrorizing killer. I had a will to live.

My next test of courage nearly wiped me out. With chemotherapy you lose your hair. When the doctors told me that I would lose my hair as a result of chemotherapy treatments, I didn't want to believe it. I set it in the back of my mind. But then it happened. As I was taking a shower, clumps of my hair came out in the palm of my hand. Panic seized me and I grew very bitter. I was crushed. I almost threw in the towel. What a price to pay just so I could live! But with the help of family and friends I managed to accept the fact that my hair was falling out. It took longer this time for me to bounce back with new courage. This condition was only temporary.

If anyone would ask me now if chemotherapy and loss of hair was worth it, I'd say yes. It was worth it. I am now in remission, and I have a new head of hair. This test of courage has strengthened my family and friends as well as myself. I feel that I am a better person as a result of my experience. I had endured what seemed like my fate. With a new outlook on life, I encourage those who are in doubt about their lives to have hope, faith, and courage.

Susan may have lost her battle, but the lives she touched during her illness help ease the pain of our loss. The many patients she talked with, helping to acquaint them with their diseases, convincing them *not* to give up, is testimony to a victory. The inner peace that she found as she searched for a purpose for the pain was also a testimony to victory.

Mrs. Glassburn, a friend from my Lioness Club, offered another testimony. Shortly after her first visit to Susan in September of 1979, she confided her feelings to me, "I was afraid. I almost turned around before I reached the door to her room. I just didn't know what I would say to her. Sickness had always frightened me."

But after that first visit Mrs. Glassburn began going on a regular every-other-week basis. "Talk about someone picking you up!" she said. "Susan had a way of always cheering *me* instead of the other way around. I always left feeling lighter and happier and always looked forward to the next visit. Such a concern for others, such a happy young woman!"

A verse from Proverbs, 18:14, best exemplifies what Susan was trying to get across to all those other patients she came in contact with: *"Your will to live can sustain you when you are sick; but if you lose it, your last hope is gone."* Perhaps, through this book, Susan's work will continue on a while longer.

After Susan's funeral, and after life had begun to return to some semblance of normalcy, I woke up one morning with a terrible feeling of despair. It seemed that Susan was upset, wondering why I had not contacted her. She couldn't reach out to me; I had to do the reaching. I thought I was losing my mind; I phoned Carolyn.

"Am I going crazy? I know Susan is dead, but I've had these feelings all morning that she is trying to tell me something."

"Just sit quietly for a while. Sit and think. Maybe an understanding will come," she advised.

When I hung up the phone, I sat at the kitchen table and let my mind wander. Suddenly I was up searching for paper and pen. I began to write notes to four of Susan's old hospital roommates. After a brief introduction, I wrote passages from two of Susan's writings to Nellie, Olive, Diana, and Dorothy:

> If you ask me if chemo and hair loss are worth it, I'd say yes. The test of courage has strengthened my family and friends and I know I am a better person as a result of my illness. I endured what looked like my fate. With a new outlook on life, I encourage those who are in doubt to have hope. "*To have hope, you must have faith. To have faith, you must have courage. To have courage, you must have a will to live.*"

> and

> Those who have goals, interests, etc., have more meaning to their lives; something to reach for, grab onto to keep going. Determination to accomplish these is really worth fighting for. Once you reach your goals, the rewards will be worth the effort.

I signed the notes and felt a sense of relief. I felt that I was carrying on Susan's job of spreading hope. One week later Diana phoned me from the hospital. "I had made up my mind to stop chemo until I read your letter," she said. "But I could hear Susan talking to me so clearly—telling me to fight," she said. She consented to further treatment. Between sick spells, she re-read Susan's writings and felt, again, Susan's urgings for her to fight against death.

"There are times when I wonder if it's all worth it, but then I think of Susan and I know even though she's gone, she won the battle," Diana said. "And I want to win too." I realized Susan's courage had become strength for others.

Because of the nature of Susan's disease, her donor request was denied. But we did the next best thing. With the help of the Linden Northeast Lioness Club and Susan's memorial fund, we established a full scholarship at the Pilot Dog's Association in Columbus in her memory. The scholarship provided a seeing-eye dog for a young woman just Susan's age. So, in a way, Susan *did* donate her eyes; her death had helped another girl to "see."

Susan's monument is a granite stone from the Black Hills. It was designed by Brenda, who is now a graduate of the Columbus School of Art and Design. It portrays three bluebirds sitting on a branch, an old wooden fence, flowers and butterflies.

Charles Schulz, the creator of Woodstock, sent us a brass replica of Susan's beloved character to be placed on her stone. To commemorate her twenty-first birthday, John carved a Woodstock from a block of cherry wood, and it sits beside her grave.

Surviving the death of a child is by far the most difficult task a parent will ever have to face. Some mornings I look in the mirror and marvel that I am still alive, while Susan is dead. I am surprised that what began as day-to-day survival following her death has slowly eased into acceptance.

Susan believed God gave her pain for a reason. As I witnessed her personality blossom, her caring ways affect others, and her internal serenity help fellow patients accept Faith as the only answer to life's problems, it was difficult not to recognize her as His

114

tool. "Faith is the substance of things hoped for, the evidence of things not seen," (Hebrews 11:1) best ex-emplifies my own outlook for the future.

I believe that Susan's soul is at peace, and that those of us who are left behind were strengthened, not broken, by sharing her last months. I believe that the agony of seeing the empty place at the table will one day cease, and that faith has helped us begin to mend.